PRAISE FOR *THE DE...*

'Shows the unstoppable rise in the use of big data and AI in large M&A deals, which mirrors every other industry, including global sports such as football. And, just as we found in the sports industry where we argue that "the machine proposes but the human decides", Driessen, Faelten and Moeller show why the human element of deals will only become more important with the increasing use of technology to conduct deals. This is a must-read for anyone engaged in divestitures, acquisitions and large financial deals.'
Chris Brady, Chief Intelligence Officer, Sportsology Group

'A insightful and thought-provoking read for those involved in mergers, acquisitions and divestitures, as well as in the world of corporate finance. As deals have become part of the DNA of business strategy, so has the use of technology in advancing and accelerating the execution of the right transactions. Through the lens of experience, the authors use interviews and stories with leading dealmakers to highlight the impact of technology on today's deal market, and to forecast the likely implications of digital transformation to the M&A process. Whether an experienced investment banker or early career analyst, you need to read *The Deal Paradox*.'
Kenneth H Marks, Managing Partner and Founder, High Rock Partners

'In a world where rapid technology development and adoption are forcing the pace of change, this book reminds us that human values and relationships are the foundation of all successful business dealings.'
Anne Glover, Chief Executive and Co-founder, Amadeus Capital

The Deal Paradox

Mergers and acquisitions success in the age of digital transformation

Michel Driessen
Anna Faelten
Scott Moeller

Publisher's note

Every possible effort has been made to ensure that the information contained in this book is accurate at the time of going to press, and the publishers and authors cannot accept responsibility for any errors or omissions, however caused. No responsibility for loss or damage occasioned to any person acting, or refraining from action, as a result of the material in this publication can be accepted by the editor, the publisher or the authors.

First published in Great Britain and the United States in 2023 by Kogan Page Limited

Apart from any fair dealing for the purposes of research or private study, or criticism or review, as permitted under the Copyright, Designs and Patents Act 1988, this publication may only be reproduced, stored or transmitted, in any form or by any means, with the prior permission in writing of the publishers, or in the case of reprographic reproduction in accordance with the terms and licences issued by the CLA. Enquiries concerning reproduction outside these terms should be sent to the publishers at the undermentioned addresses:

2nd Floor, 45 Gee Street	8 W 38th Street, Suite 902	4737/23 Ansari Road
London	New York, NY 10018	Daryaganj
EC1V 3RS	USA	New Delhi 110002
United Kingdom		India

www.koganpage.com

Kogan Page books are printed on paper from sustainable forests.

© Michel Driessen, Anna Faelten and Scott Moeller, 2023

The rights of Michel Driessen, Anna Faelten and Scott Moeller to be identified as the authors of this work has been asserted by them in accordance with the Copyright, Designs and Patents Act 1988.

ISBNs
Hardback   978 1 3986 0813 9
Paperback   978 1 3986 0811 5
Ebook   978 1 3986 0812 2

British Library Cataloguing-in-Publication Data
A CIP record for this book is available from the British Library.

Library of Congress Cataloging-in-Publication Data
Names: Driessen, Michel, author. | Faelten, Anna, author. | Moeller, Scott, author.
Title: The deal paradox : mergers and acquisitions success in the age of
  digital transformation / Michel Driessen, Anna Faelten, Scott Moeller.
Description: London, United Kingdom ; New York, NY : Kogan Page, 2023. |
  Includes bibliographical references and index.
Identifiers: LCCN 2022052786 (print) | LCCN 2022052787 (ebook) | ISBN
  9781398608115 (paperback) | ISBN 9781398608139 (hardback) | ISBN
  9781398608122 (ebook)
Subjects: LCSH: Consolidation and merger of corporations. | Deals. | BISAC:
  BUSINESS & ECONOMICS / Mergers & Acquisitions
Classification: LCC HD2746.5 .D74 2023 (print) | LCC HD2746.5 (ebook) |
  DDC 658.1/62–dc23/eng/20221104
LC record available at https://lccn.loc.gov/2022052786
LC ebook record available at https://lccn.loc.gov/2022052787

Typeset by Integra Software Services, Pondicherry
Print production managed by Jellyfish
Printed and bound by CPI Group (UK) Ltd, Croydon, CR0 4YY

*To my parents Coen (1934–2015) and Alda (1936–2020)
who encouraged me to think big.*
MD

To my wonderful children, Valentin and Vilma.
AF

*To my wife Daniela and my children Christine, Andrew,
Ellen and Jonathan.*
SM

CONTENTS

Acknowledgements xi

Introduction: Do deals or die 1
The automation paradox parallel 1
Defining our terms: what and who's in a deal? 3
The rising pressure to do deals 4
The paradox thickens: do humans really matter more? 6
No going back: how the pandemic changed deals forever 7
Technology to the rescue 9
About the authors 13
Chapter by chapter, blow by blow 14
References 18

1 Strategy or bust 21
Technology triggers deals 22
The relationship between strategy and dealmaking 23
The strategy paradox 25
Behavioural factors 27
The dangerous human 30
Does opportunity eat strategy for breakfast? 33
From theory to practice: strategy in action 35
References 41

2 Identify your target 45
No going back: the multi-dimensional, moving target range 46
A new dimension in dealmaking 47
The perfect environment for technology 48
Technology to the rescue: platforms are smarter than people 52
From theory to practice: the views of a leading innovator 56
Black Swan, White Swan – how social data is the new gold 59

A tech fund leader with vision 60
Summing up: power to the people 64
References 65

3 Winning hearts, minds and money 67

Setting out terms 68
The key drivers 68
The role of technology 70
Standardization clears the runway to success 70
The enduring role of the adviser 74
Boosting the bids: adding value in auctions 76
Taking care of baby: selling a highly personal business 77
The role of negotiation and who does it best 80
The machine that negotiates 81
References 87

4 Priced to perfection 89

The gap between value and price 91
Through the looking glass: the vagaries of valuation 92
Don't forget deal costs 95
Using technology to power pricing 96
The art of the deal price 101
The future of pricing 104
References 107

5 Taking care of business 109

What can go wrong will go wrong: when due diligence fails 110
Know the rules: regulation and due diligence 111
Disruption and the age of due diligence 112
The need for speed and the value of going slow 113
More haste, more speed: using technology to square the circle 114
Soft factors, hard landings: taking a more rounded view 118
The role of technology in due diligence 119
The inside track on data: a view from the virtual coal face 124
Summing up 129
References 131

6 Selling the story 133

The rise and fail of the corporate storyteller 134
Can you hear me? Why communication is getting tougher 137
Clear and simple: how the professionals do it 142
Summing up: comms technology makes people stand out 147
References 150

7 After the deal 151

Not so fast: the complications of integration 152
Two sides of the coin: integration winners and losers 153
Adding grist to the mill: the barriers to integration 155
Technology and the human touch 160
Testing our case 164
Going for gold: the people's eye view 168
The technologist bytes back 170
Summing up 172
References 173

Conclusion: The future of the deal 175

Why deals will remain vital 175
How deals will be done in the future 180
Deal technology and the human factor 182
The future deal process stage by stage 183
Who will do deals in the future? 188
Summing up 193
References 196

Index 197

ACKNOWLEDGEMENTS

We are indebted to a large number of people in developing the idea for this book and producing it. First, Brian Thompson from Lang Communications, who has helped us from inception to completion and everywhere in between, and his colleague Paul Sylvester for additional support.

At Kogan Page, we are grateful for the production and editorial support of a big team, but mostly to Isabelle Cheng, Anne-Marie Heeney, Susi Lowndes and Ryan Norman.

Michel and Anna are thankful for EY LLP's support while allowing them both the time and editorial freedom to work on this project. Scott would like to thank Bayes Business School, City, University of London for the same.

An important aspect of this book – and, we believe, its unique benefit – comes from the combined wisdom of a large number of senior executives and industry observers who have shared their stories, thoughts and predictions with us, bringing to life what could otherwise be dry material. Their names appear in each of the relevant chapters, but bear repeating here, Ashish Agarwal, Andrew Binsted, Anthony Byrne, Paul Davison, Ben Harrison, Steve King, Ross Heritage, Carrie-Anne Holt, Rob Lawson, Lucy Legh, Stephen Malthouse, Adrian Moorhouse, Tony Qui, Martin Rand and Chris Salt. We also would like to thank SS&C Intralinks and Bayes Business School for providing some of the underlying data that made sure our hypotheses about the M&A market were borne out by facts.

Finally, each of us is grateful to our families and their understanding when we have spent time researching, discussing and writing (and rewriting) this book instead of being with them. This includes Anna's second child, Vilma, born around the same time as our book entered the final stages of the printing process.

Introduction: Do deals or die

Why people matter more in the age of automation, what the pandemic taught us about human nature, and how deal technology may only just be getting started

Let's start by unpacking exactly what we mean by the term deal paradox and, by doing so, bring to the surface the key questions this book aims to raise. Then we'll briefly take you, chapter by chapter, through how we will set about answering them.

The automation paradox parallel

Some readers may already have connected the term deal paradox with its better-known relation, the automation paradox. That goes back to the days when intelligent 'robots' were introduced to factory production. While the fear was that huge numbers of jobs would be destroyed, the reality often proved entirely different. Not only did those robots need to be designed and built by people – they also needed installing, repairing and checking by humans. In many cases, instead of reducing the number of jobs, automation actually increased them. The people involved, rather than being devalued by the advance of technology, often became more, not less, important because they moved up the value chain – from spending most of their time carrying out routine and repetitive work, to overseeing those same processes and determining ways to do those jobs better.

The parallel between the automation and deal paradox seems, initially at least, clear. As global dealmakers increasingly adopt new technology to help them identify alternative strategies, select target companies, conduct faster and more extensive due diligence and even integrate the two companies more effectively, some parts of the deal process previously undertaken by humans are being automated. Dealmakers, liberated from tasks such as endless research and number crunching, can therefore focus their attention on where they are most effective, from building trust and relationships to adding value and creatively reimagining the future. Instead of eliminating the human factor, technology is empowering it and, just as we saw with the automation paradox, is giving dealmakers the opportunity to move further up the value chain.

Mind the gap: every deal is different

While the parallel with the automation paradox appears powerful, there are also some differences. The M&A process is far less uniform than any factory floor, with every deal essentially a one-off that typically involves millions or even billions of dollars and impacts the lives of thousands of employees (often in different countries/geographies). At the top of organizations, dealmaking has always been a more personal process, built on the relationships and interactions between a buyer and a seller. In a company sale, for example, a founder may be selling his or her life's work and the buyer's board and chief executive officer (CEO) will be staking their reputations on the success of the deal. But the number of people affected goes way beyond the owners of the two companies and is typically much more important to a larger number of people than the mere automation of an industrial process, as critical as that may sometimes be to the competitive position of a company.

M&A deals are also more hit and miss. Continuing research by one of the co-authors reveals that only around half of all deals are successful (Moeller and Brady, 2014), a finding supported by numerous other studies, suggesting that technology has the potential to go beyond increasing efficiencies and can help dealmakers do better deals which generate better outcomes for all parties. To take one example from just one aspect of the deal: armed with more extensive information on potential acquisitions, gathered and analysed instantly by advanced technologies, the acquirer may be more likely to choose the right target, thereby eliminating one of the first hurdles along the multi-faced obstacle race that is the deal process.

So, while the one-off, individual nature of each deal can present a barrier to more widespread automation, the overall impact of the deal, with its great value and potentially high failure rate, makes those barriers worth overcoming.

Defining our terms: what and who's in a deal?

So, in the context of this book, what do we mean by deals and dealmakers? Obviously, mergers, acquisitions, and divestitures (as one company's divestiture is another's acquisition) would be within our definition of dealmaking, as would initial public offerings (IPOs), or indeed any tool used to provide the growth funding of an organization such as the use of Special Purpose Acquisition Companies (SPACs).

As for the 'who' of dealmakers, we include everyone from trade buyers and private equity groups to advisers, including corporate financiers, lawyers, accountants and the many types of specialist consultants whose expertise is called on at any or every stage of the deal process.

Deal technology: where we are now

We are already seeing global dealmakers adopting new technological tools such as virtual diligence, virtual data rooms (already accepted as the norm by most practitioners), natural language processing (NLP) and big data analytics to select targets and conduct more extensive due diligence. These tools make it possible to analyse vast amounts of structured and unstructured data in real time, speeding up deal processes and better identifying hidden risks. Although many dealmakers are only just beginning to integrate these tools into their daily operations, the visible gain in their long-term efficiencies is encouraging the broader M&A market to put technology at the centre of dealmaking in the coming years.

Let's not forget that new technologies can also extend into the physical world of dealmaking. For example, the use of drones to conduct due diligence is now commonplace. These drones not only make it possible to have virtual tours in factories and access locations that were almost impossible (or prohibitively expensive) to go to before, but can also be more cost-effective and efficient, thus allowing for a deeper and more detailed due diligence process.

The rising pressure to do deals

The potential of technology to support dealmakers has never been more important. Put simply, since the 2007–2008 financial crisis, companies have never been under more pressure to do deals, as demonstrated in the consistently high volume of deals since the recovery from that recession. We will examine the reasons more fully later in the book but, in a nutshell, the markets in which companies operate are changing ever more rapidly – whether driven to do so by new technologies, changing customer behaviours or the need to respond to the demands of everything from sustainability to better corporate governance and greater diversity and inclusion. And we can almost guarantee that the next few years will bring further changes that we haven't anticipated, just as early 2022 brought a war in Europe that was in no one's scenario planning a year earlier, and with it the significant impacts on energy markets, supply chains and inflation, to mention just some of the major areas that have been affected.

As a result, there is simply less time to adapt, let alone grow, organically. Instead, companies have increasingly looked to acquire the capabilities they need in order to succeed, often from start-up or early-stage companies who have been more nimble in their development and response to the above drivers. This has also contributed to the significant increase in dealmaking.

Of course, from global pandemics to wars and from interest rate rises to economic recessions, there will always be short-term factors that can put a brake on deal activity (although it is worth noting that deals can be driven just as much by 'negative' factors as 'positive' ones). For example, global supply chain problems led many companies to make acquisitions that would help them secure vital parts or commodities closer to home.

It's worth noting that this increase is not just in the big headline deals that are covered in the media. More small- and medium-sized companies are also doing deals – and not just from being the target – as many small- and mid-cap companies are increasingly looking beyond their immediate local competitors to carry out, for example, cross-border transactions.

Additionally, as technology becomes crucial to every industry, companies are increasingly looking beyond their own sectors for acquisitions to improve their own technology standing. As far back as 2015, Lloyd Blankfein, the CEO of investment banking firm Goldman Sachs, referred to the bank as 'a technology company'. This wasn't a bold boast, as *Business Insider* reported at the time that Goldman Sachs had more programmers and engineers than Facebook (Marino, 2015). This is not limited to Goldman Sachs as we have seen not just financial services firms making myriad acquisitions of technology companies; the same is happening in just about every industry from healthcare to mining. There will be a number of examples of this throughout the book, starting with the next chapter on strategy.

The need for speed

Not only do more companies want to transact more deals, they need to do them faster. That's because, with acquirers under pressure to find the right targets, competition is intense and sellers in so-called hot sectors are increasingly calling the shots. With the need to get more deals done more quickly, and with experienced dealmakers and advisers in short supply, deal technology has the potential to plug the gaps.

More speed, more deals, more risk. The case for deal technology to improve analysis, speed up processes and reduce that risk is clear. Throughout our book we will be looking at how it is being applied, its current advantages and the potential for these to become even more valuable in the future. But this is not a tech-heavy text (which anyway would likely soon become out of date because of the speed at which new technologies are being developed) as our real focus won't be on the tools themselves but on how they impact the deal process and the dealmakers. That said, we will be mentioning some of these innovative tools as we go along.

The paradox thickens: do humans really matter more?

As new technologies like artificial intelligence (AI) make it possible for machines to take on more complex and, dare we say, human tasks, the nature of the deal paradox takes a different shape: could technology, rather than taking the burden of repetitive tasks to free up humans, actually be better at some of those more complex, non-linear, intuitive tasks traditionally considered best left to people? If that seems a little too sci-fi for a business book, consider that just about every task previously regarded as being the sole domain of humans, from playing poker to selecting which professional baseball players to sign, has apparently been proven to be better done by machines. In the case of baseball players, the book *Moneyball* (Lewis, 2004) outlined how hard stats not gut instinct were key to acquiring the best – and sometimes cheapest – players.

Interestingly, both poker and baseball player transfer negotiations have stereotypically been seen as the preserve of tight-lipped alpha males capable of taking big risks without blinking. They are also areas where being the sole source of authority and information is seen as the ultimate key to success. Technology can work against that, being more dependent on the sharing and pooling of data, supporting the ability to work together across offices and borders. That could mean greater demand for more collaborative dealmakers working outside traditional office hierarchies and could lead to a much more diverse set of individuals throughout the dealmaking food chain. Contributing to this is the rise of working from home, helping those that might have been excluded from the heat of the deal – due to childcare, disability or even simply a more introverted nature – to have a place at the table. Taking that one step further, those currently put off by what we might call the 'traditional deal culture' may be more attracted to the profession in the future, changing the dynamics and thereby improving the results.

Or is there change ahead that will fundamentally alter the very nature of the deal process itself? If, for example, technology allows us instant access to all the information we need, verified as being true through blockchain technology or an equivalent, could an entire stage of the deal process, in this case due diligence, one day be removed or at least greatly reduced in complexity?

Alongside the current practical applications of deal technology, we'll be examining these broader themes and then offering our conclusions and predictions.

While these sorts of questions can seem challenging, they often boil down to a simple question. What are the essential human qualities that remain vital to the dealmaking process and which cannot be replaced by machines?

No going back: how the pandemic changed deals forever

Albeit in the most difficult and devastating circumstances, the global Covid-19 pandemic offered a rare and, we sincerely hope, never to be repeated, opportunity to explore this question. Before we lay out our findings, please note that this isn't a book about the pandemic, but we are exploring it here because we believe its impact on dealmaking has been – and will continue to be – significant and long-lasting.

As every reader will recall, the early stages of the pandemic saw strict lockdowns imposed across the world, bringing deal activity, especially large deals, to a near-total standstill in early 2020. One study by BCG (Kengelbach et al, 2020) showed that for deals over

$500 million, the typical monthly volume is around 50 deals. This had risen to over 90 deals per month in 2019 but dropped to less than 20 in February and March of 2020 as the Covid-19 pandemic hit. Even that low number was only likely achievable because much of the work had been done before the pandemic started. Obviously, economic uncertainty on a huge and unprecedented scale was the key reason for this stasis but it was also driven by the belief that, with dealmakers unable to travel and meet in person, deals simply could not take place.

This was based on the assumption that, as history had thus far dictated, something as hugely significant and intensely personal as one company acquiring (or partnering or merging with) another could not be done until the buyer and seller had a physical connection where they could 'look each other in the eye', 'see the whites of each other's eyes', 'press the flesh' or 'shake on it'. Bearing in mind that these 'vital' in-person meetings often extend beyond the C-suite to include key managers, customers, distributors and suppliers, this meant a lot of meeting and greeting.

Even the physical aspects of the deal were regarded as needing the human touch with, under normal circumstances, buyers insisting that they must visit factories, offices and other locations in order to 'kick the tyres' before completion. It was not uncommon to find a business leader mentioning their 'gut feel' in trumpeting a deal because he or she felt a personal connection with the other company and the key people involved.

Do deals or die: the crucible of change

As the lockdowns continued into 2021, dealmakers were facing a simple choice – challenge and overcome those conventions or simply do no deals. Tough choices, but in the end a 'deal or die' attitude prevailed over 'doing things as we've always done'.

What undoubtedly helped this decision was that, although the pandemic had removed many of the elements of human interaction deemed essential for dealmaking, it had added to the pressure to do deals. Some companies, for example, needed to acquire new digital processes at pace and adopt new technologies to cope with social distancing and lockdowns. Other companies, deprived of income during the pandemic, needed to divest assets to raise money. So, under ever greater pressure to do deals at a time when dealmaking appeared impossible, the crucible of change was heating up, melting even the most long-held and solidly formed assumptions.

Passing the sniff test: the meeting that never happened

An example from one of our authors perfectly illustrates the conundrum facing dealmakers. A multimillion-pound deal was stalling as the UK-based investor could not agree an acquisition until they had met the seller in person, despite the seemingly insurmountable barrier of strict lockdowns. Our author tried to identify what human sense needed to be satisfied by the investor. Clearly, both parties could see each other on video calls and all the deal information had been presented and verified electronically. The only thing our author could identify as missing was smell and touch. Could that be the key? A socially distanced outdoor meeting in a park was suggested, but the buyer investor eventually relented and agreed to proceed with investigating the merits of the deal online. No insight was provided as to the investor's change of mind but perhaps it was the 'secret service' nature of the proposed physical encounter in a location where no one would observe that they were breaking lockdown rules. But if it had gone ahead perhaps one of you, reading these words, may finally understand why they saw two serious-looking business people sniffing each other on benches in St James Park or any other of London's distinguished public green spaces.

Technology to the rescue

Instead, as we know, technology stepped into the breach, replacing physical meetings with video calls and substituting site visits with drone surveillance. Unable to travel and meet, dealmakers were more open to using the technology and data that lay at their fingertips, but had previously been underused.

Human behaviours also changed. As video calls took us into people's homes during a time of crisis, bonds were strengthened rather than weakened as we sometimes learned more about each other than in any formal setting ever before.

That was important, because those all-important feelings of human connection and trust were even more vital at a time when deals could not be signed in person. Culture was also reshaping. People who thrived in formal settings and office all-nighters found themselves having to learn new skills, while some of those formerly in the shadows emerged to reveal new strengths. Of course, the impact of this new technology wasn't always positive as analysts and associates at investment banks, for example, complained of always being on call, and for many there was a personal space intrusion due to the lack of an ability to separate work and home.

While we'll examine these views in more detail and explore the evidence to support or disprove them, there is one fact that is already incontestable. Despite lockdowns continuing on and off throughout 2021, deal numbers hit record highs.

In fact, the total value of global dealmaking breached $5 trillion for the first time in 2021, up 64 per cent from a year earlier. There were 64,000 deals, up 24 per cent from 2020 (Toole, 2022) and higher than the non-pandemic-affected 2019. And many of the countries hardest hit by the pandemic saw the most deal growth, led by the United States.

It's also worth noting that technology deals exceeded $1 trillion for the first time ever in 2021, up 71 per cent from the previous year (Krueger, 2022). Interestingly, tech deal activity spanned across all levels of the market, from small start-ups being bought for their intellectual property (IP) rights through to mega-deals, as well-funded, high-growth companies sought to expand into new markets, buy into new technologies or acquire new talent.

The genie is out of the bottle

Yet many of these changes were already on their way even before Covid-19: the pandemic was the catalyst, not the cause. Video conferencing, for example, had been showcased by AT&T as early as the 1964/1965 New York World's Fair (Darlin, 2014). Its great-grandchildren, Zoom and Microsoft Teams, for example, were already available and in use, albeit by very few people, long before Covid-19 spread across the world. This highlights an important point relevant to our whole book, namely that technology adoption is often gradual, sometimes frustratingly slow – and then suddenly takes off as a new use case becomes the catalyst for the sudden explosion.

MAPPING THE RISE OF DEAL TECHNOLOGY

Prior to the pandemic, the use of virtual data rooms – secure online repositories for document storage and distribution during the deal process – was already well established. However, with less opportunity for physical meeting and deal numbers rising, they were used much more extensively during the pandemic. Figure 0.1, from global technology provider SS&C Intralinks, shows the average data volume per data room over time.

FIGURE 0.1 Average number of pages per virtual data room

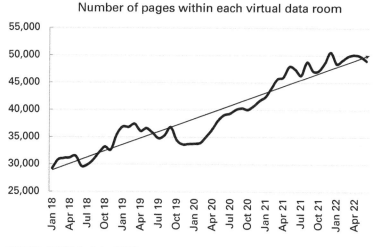

SOURCE SS&C Intralinks, 2022

> Note how the volume not only rises steeply during the pandemic lockdown period but remains high after it, even during a period when deal numbers began to tail off. This endorses our view that once the genie is out of the bottle, the stopper is blown away. 'The pandemic accelerated the use of deal technology and demonstrated its value, enabling dealmakers to focus more of their time on the people elements where they can add most value. We don't see this as a temporary response but likely a permanent shift,' explains Ken Bisconti, co-head of SS&C Intralinks.

While there is a natural tendency to look at the benefits of technology primarily in terms of efficiency gains, this is changing as its impact becomes transformational, sometimes in unexpected ways. One example came during the merger of two major multinational companies (and fierce competitors) during the pandemic. A participant reflected to one of the authors afterwards that the smooth nature of the deal process, which included agreement on highly sensitive areas such as the post-merger management structure, was in no small part due to the fact that meetings were held virtually. The reason? Our source's theory was that the equal screen space afforded to each meeting participant on video calls made it harder for dominant egos to hijack or own the agenda. A small difference but a major unintended consequence.

This reflects the underlying tensions between traditional, ingrained approaches and new ways of operating, which had been bubbling under the surface for years. Aided by technology, the lamp has now been rubbed and the genie is finally out of the bottle. The repercussions – from deal culture and the types of characters who have traditionally dominated the dealmaking landscape, to AI and machine learning (ML) that anticipates problems and sparks new ideas – will be felt for years to come.

Getting on the right side of this change will be crucial for any future deal success. Whether you are a business leader, adviser, acquirer, target or technologist, this book will help you to lead the market, not follow it. For those who can do so, the opportunities are simply immense. For example, market disruption, new technologies and the rapidly increasing levels of environmental awareness are all accelerating change and making deals the best route for companies to get ahead and stay there. Based on stories, interviews with key players and the authors' many years of dealmaking experience, *The Deal Paradox* will show you how.

About the authors

Between them, Michel Driessen, Anna Faelten and Scott Moeller have clocked up decades of dealmaking experience, built on landmark deals ranging from Morgan Stanley's IPO at the height of the 1980s banking boom and Kraft's bittersweet takeover of Cadbury in 2009 as the world emerged from recession, to key tech deals including building the £1 billion financial data intelligence company Acuris (formerly Mergermarket) which ultimately sold to ION in 2019.

The authors' first book together, *Why Deals Fail & How to Rescue Them*, was published by Profile Books in their *Economist* book series to wide acclaim in 2016.

Michel is a senior partner in global professional services firm EY's Strategy and Transactions group and focuses on complex and international transactions for large corporates and private equity firms in the Consumer Products and Retail sectors.

Anna leads EY's Technology, Media and Telecoms (TMT) Corporate Finance practice, working with high-growth technology companies and investors.

Scott is Professor in the Practice of Finance at Bayes Business School, City, University of London and is the founder and director of its M&A Research Centre. Other than being a prolific author, market commentator and teacher, he has had a long banking career that included time with Morgan Stanley, Deutsche Bank and JPMorgan in New York, Tokyo, Frankfurt and London.

Together, their passion for dealmaking is contagious and has won them the trust of leading industry figures who share their stories and insights throughout this book. Michel, Anna and Scott will present dealmaking from the perspective of current practitioners who know all the detail but are also capable of stepping back to see the big picture. After all, deals have one thing in common with books – you have to sell the story – and this book will cover every twist and turn of the dealmaking process.

Chapter by chapter, blow by blow

The book is structured to reflect the dealmaking process, from setting out the strategy and identifying the right target through to the integration of the two businesses.

Along the way, we'll introduce readers to the new dealmaking landscape and show how technology has also acted as a diversity enabler, breaking down barriers in terms of the deals done and the people involved in them.

Our argument will be illustrated and informed by interviews with those top dealmakers who will share their stories, triumphs and challenges in this new and emerging deal world. And, critically, we'll also be asking them, 'What's next?'.

Chapter 1

We begin with *Strategy or bust*, talking to the former global head of M&A at energy giant BP, Rob Lawson, who explains how deals are absolutely key to their strategic transformation to becoming an integrated energy company. We examine how the deal rationale really starts with understanding where a business is today, where it wants to go and how a deal can help get them there faster. Crucially we look at whether these big strategic calls can only be made by leaders or whether human weaknesses such as overconfidence are the road to ruin and need to be eliminated from the process by technology. We also draw on the latest data and insight on technology-driven trends and how they impact dealmaking, lifting the lid on how it is blurring sector boundaries. Real-life examples of businesses that reinvented themselves through strategic acquisitions support our argument that dealmaking is increasingly becoming the most important tool in a business leader's toolbox.

Chapter 2

Having made dealmaking a lynchpin in your growth strategy, it's time to *Identify your target*. We talk to Paul Davison, partner at venture capital fund SoftBank Vision Fund, about how he uses technology and people to identify targets that are under the radar and represent better value for investors. In fact, the use of technologies has become a gamechanger, putting greater power in the hands of acquirers and opening up a whole new world of possibilities, particularly for those previously without the experience or resources to find opportunities. In addition, we talk to the founder of a technology platform that uses big data to find new target companies and understand the flow of capital within sectors to gain a better understanding of the deal landscape. We also get the inside track from experienced data analysts who explain how human behaviour is still very much part of the deal picture, no matter how tech-driven the deal process.

Chapter 3

Few deals are completed by one person and their bank balance. Typically, targets and investors need to be won over, requiring human connections as well as financial facts. Here, our innate desire for personal engagement can work alongside powerful data in the journey to *Winning hearts, minds and money*. As key financial metrics become more standardized, technology makes it easier for buyers to grasp the true value of a business. But – particularly in a sellers' market – buyers must also hit the right emotional notes to close the deal. In contrast, we hear from a tech leader who believes the best route to successful negotiation is by taking humans out of the equation almost entirely and replacing them with his company's custom-built AI-powered technology. We look at examples of what works and what does not in getting deals over the line, highlighting the value of relationships – a reminder that, ultimately, people are still persuaded by people, not technology.

Chapter 4

We go on to discuss the critical aspect of valuation in *Priced to perfection*, looking at how to avoid paying too much, even in red-hot sectors, but also examining the flip side of this in terms of showing sellers how to maximize their value. We examine the difference between price and value, along the way answering the age-old question, how can you get more for less? Technology has a key and growing role here, with new, AI-driven software promising to marry the human art of pricing with a data-driven approach, cutting out the to-ing and fro-ing to find the sweet spot of price agreement straightaway. Crucially, we consider whether the ability to bargain is an essential human trait that lies at the heart of dealmaking or something where emotion and relationships need to be replaced – or at least complemented – by technology.

Chapter 5

In *Taking care of business*, we look at the area of any deal that often takes the most time and, together with the topic of Chapter 7, has the biggest impact on its success, yet the mere mention of it can cure insomnia at a stroke: due diligence. The bad news here is that as deal numbers rise and the pressure to get them quickly over the line intensifies, this is going to be an ever-growing area of work. But the good news is that technology can shoulder more and more of the heavy lifting, allowing dealmakers to do what they do best: build trust and add value to get deals agreed and completed. We hear from Ashish Agarwal, former senior vice president, strategy and corporate development at global computer security software company McAfee and explore how, by using tech tools and data, companies are not only carrying out due diligence faster and more efficiently, they are creating opportunities to do better deals. And finally we find out where this is all heading – what's the next frontier for deal-assisting technology in due diligence?

Chapter 6

From persuading investors to back a deal to getting staff in the new entity to work together successfully after completion, communication is key. What that comes down to, ultimately, is *Selling the story*. As we'll learn, stories are a powerful and uniquely human tool, requiring a simple, engaging message delivered from a trusted source. We'll talk to experts at a leading financial communications agency about how technology is helping them to get their messages across more quickly and effectively and generate greater insight about their effectiveness. But what about the flip side? In a multichannel, technology-empowered, always-on world, is it harder for companies and their communications advisers to control the narrative? We also look at how the trend towards more direct communications could disrupt deal communications.

Chapter 7

In the heat of the deal, it's easy to forget that the real measure of its success lies *After the deal*, so in this chapter we feature examples of when corporates tie the knot – from happy ever afters to nightmare honeymoons. We examine the likely roadblocks to a successful merger of two companies, from IT systems to people and cultures. This is an area that has traditionally been very high on human touch but some believe the most critical part of integration is now between technology systems, not humans. So, we test that hypothesis, first by hearing from Olympic gold medallist-turned talent development guru Adrian Moorhouse about how he successfully brings together the two pre-deal 'tribes' in post-deal integration. Then we hear from a technologist who grapples with marrying together different enterprise systems after the deal. To find out how that worked in practice, we interview the key players involved in overseeing and advising on a series of complex, high-value tech acquisitions.

Conclusion

Our final chapter, *The future of the deal*, discusses how the authors apply their own experience to forecast how the future will change:

- **Why** deals will remain vital.
- **How** deals will be done.
- **Who** will do deals.

We also preview the future through the eyes of the pioneers, from those blazing a trail with new AI-driven technology to those who envision a new kind of more diverse dealmaker. We examine which stage of the deal process is currently most impacted and look ahead to the next wave of technology-led disruption and how it will shape the deal landscape for decades to come. We think big about what that will mean for our industry and how legacy dealmakers will have to adapt as a new generation comes to the fore.

We can't promise that it will be a smooth ride ahead, but after reading this book we hope you will find it a more interesting and profitable journey.

References

Darlin, D (2014) How the future looked in 1964: the picturephone, *The New York Times*, 26 June, www.nytimes.com/2014/06/27/upshot/how-the-future-looked-in-1964-the-picturephone.html (archived at https://perma.cc/NW8W-SZ93)

Kengelbach, J, Keienburg, G, Degen, D, Söllner, T, Kashyrkin, A and Sievers, S (2020) The 2020 M&A report: alternative deals gain traction. Boston Consulting Group, 29 September, www.bcg.com/publications/2020/mergers-acquisitions-report-alternative-deals-gain-traction (archived at https://perma.cc/W34G-55UH)

Krueger, A (2022) A record year for technology M&A – what's behind the boom? Allen & Overy, 12 January, www.allenovery.com/en-gb/global/news-and-insights/publications/a-record-year-for-technology-ma-whats-behind-the-boom (archived at https://perma.cc/5MC6-88UK)

Lewis, M (2004) *Moneyball*, W.W. Norton & Company, New York

Marino, J (2015) Goldman Sachs is a tech company, *Business Insider*, 12 April, www.businessinsider.in/finance/goldman-sachs-is-a-tech-company/articleshow/46897984.cms (archived at https://perma.cc/E25K-2YLA)

Moeller, S and Brady, C (2014) *Intelligent M&A: Navigating the mergers and acquisitions minefield* (2nd edition), John Wiley and Sons, Chichester

Toole, M (2022) Dealmakers ring out 2021 as the year of M&A, *Refinitiv*, 12 January, www.refinitiv.com/perspectives/market-insights/dealmakers-ring-out-2021-as-the-year-of-ma/ (archived at https://perma.cc/3N7W-LQJM)

1

Strategy or bust

Why human instinct can be both the best and worst strategic tool in a disrupted, deal-driven world

As highlighted in our introduction to this book, more and more companies are turning to M&A as a means to advance growth plans and enact strategy.

While factors such as interest rates and access to funding are often identified as key drivers for M&A activity, the simpler and more powerful reason is that companies are facing the need to adjust to huge changes, both externally and internally – and the pace at which these changes are taking place is accelerating. This is not just about the need, for example to be at the cutting edge of developments within their industry, but also to digitize, prepare for a low-carbon world and keep pace with the social concerns of diversity and inclusion.

That is a very tough task. It makes the decision to acquire a company that already has some of the required skills in place – be it intellectual property, technologies or customers – an increasingly effective way to advance corporate strategy. Or to put it in economic terms, company boards and senior management have determined that the significant costs and risks of acquiring a business through M&A are outweighed by the potential benefits.

Technology triggers deals

As we noted in the introductory chapter, back in 2015, Goldman Sachs CEO Lloyd Blankfein said of the bank he headed: 'We are a technology firm' (Marino, 2015). He wasn't announcing that they were now the new Microsoft or Apple; what he meant was that the way they did business would now be through technology, both within the bank in terms of risk and control systems, and externally in terms of how Goldman Sachs engaged with customers, including the design, sales and support of new financial products.

That technology focus was a key plank to their global strategy – and a critical way to enact it was through buying companies that owned and developed the technology they needed. For example, in the year following Lloyd Blankfein's statement, Goldman Sachs bought spreadsheet software company ClearFactr to help improve financial modelling (Peyton, 2018). Fast-forward to the 2020s and Goldman Sachs are still deploying the same tactic to advance their strategy, with their focus currently on both investing in and acquiring cloud, AI and cybersecurity capabilities. Yes, they can try to develop these skills in-house, but usually that route is too slow for the fast changes required in the business and especially to keep ahead, or at least on par with, some of the often nimbler new fintech companies trying to expand into some of the most profitable niches of the banking ecosystem.

It's a similar story across many other industries. For example:

- In pharmaceuticals, DNA-related discoveries and new technologies that revolutionize patient treatment mean that, despite their own huge internal research and development (R&D) investments, big pharma cannot keep up without making acquisitions.
- The automotive industry has seen a major technology and manufacturing shift away first from diesel engines, then to hybrid and now to fully electric cars. But technology isn't stopping there, with the anticipation that further changes will perhaps be needed to develop efficient hydrogen motors. These changes would incorporate not just the new technology within each car or truck, but also the delivery

mechanisms to get the 'fuel' (whether that be petrol, electricity or hydrogen) quickly and reliably to each driver when they need it.
- In the technology sector itself, the 'war for talent' is so intense that so-called 'aqui-hires' are becoming increasingly common, whereby a business is acquired solely or predominantly to gain access to a world-class development team.
- The consumer products sector is applying technologies to understand customer behaviours and trends better and in more detail. Plus, new technologies provide these companies with the opportunity to sell more products and services online or develop entire new distribution channels and ecosystems (e.g. the Metaverse).

And as if industry wasn't facing enough change with its own sector-specific factors, some changes transcend industry. Sustainability is perhaps the perfect example because it isn't just an issue for companies in carbon-related industries such as the automotive sector just mentioned. The demands of moving to a lower carbon footprint globally are adding another technology layer for all companies in any industry.

Amid the growing glare of investor and consumer interest in climate change, many companies are now reassessing their strategies in light of the need to reduce carbon emissions, and those companies that are still ignoring this issue are doing so at their own peril. Later in this chapter, we'll hear from someone right at the centre of this storm, charged with doing the deals that will help steer a global 'supertanker' towards a low- or no-carbon future.

The relationship between strategy and dealmaking

Even if we take the simplest definition of strategy, which we would define as 'identifying how we will win', it's clear that deals are becoming an increasingly vital way of achieving that strategy. Of course, acquisition – that is, buying another company outright – is not the only route here. Mergers, strategic alliances and joint ventures are all options, combining talents and technologies to tackle the future. Or management can decide to make a minority (but significant) investment in another company that has the skills that it needs. Perhaps the most common way of implementing a strategy is through organic growth, considered by many managers as perhaps the best and cheapest route, with no need for expensive and financially complex acquisitions and the inherently difficult integration process that follows. But the flip side of that argument is that, with time pressing more heavily than ever and changes taking place at an ever-faster pace, why wait to grow a new branch when you can buy the whole tree?

It says something about the speed of change today that even the most successful and fastest-growing companies can now seemingly no longer solely rely simply on their organic growth.

> **APPLE DEAL TO BUY BEATS HITS THE HIGH NOTES**
>
> Back in 2014, when Apple decided to focus more attention on the audio aspects of its industry-leading iPhone (with 2 billion products already sold) (Sohail, 2021), many expected it to rely on its own hugely talented technology teams, backed up by a vast cash war chest. Instead, it went out and bought iconic headphone company Beats Electronics for $3 billion, at a stroke giving Apple the capabilities it needed (Chen, 2014). It's a deal that hit the right note then and still sounds good today with an estimated 100 million AirPods sold annually (Espósito, 2022) and this doesn't even include the continued sale of the 'traditional' over-the-ear headphones that had made Beats famous.

This demonstrates that today's fast-paced world doesn't allow the time for companies to develop new and often highly complex capabilities in-house. Indeed, attempting to do it yourself will frequently be the riskier strategy – with acquisition the best and often only option, even with the accompanying challenges that we will discuss in the different chapters of this book. These include conducting due diligence, determining the right deal price, and the difficulties of effectively and efficiently integrating the acquisition into the buyer without losing the capabilities that drove the acquisition in the first place.

You may note here that we are not describing M&A as being a strategy in itself. That's because it isn't. Strategy is a company's vision for the future, but to be successful it must include a road map to get there. Think of strategy in terms of deciding to travel from, say, London to Edinburgh. Options might include taking the plane, train, bus or driving, and if driving, whether to take your own car or hire someone to take you there. Those alternatives are the tactic to achieve the strategy. And in M&A terms, doing a deal is the equivalent of taking an Uber along one part of that route or indeed the entire way. Taking an Uber isn't the strategy, but it enables you to achieve that strategy. Similarly, an oil company buying a wind farm company is the tactic to support the overall strategy of transforming the business away from a carbon-based oil and gas exploration and production company.

The strategy paradox

Having put that straight, let's jump to our central thesis, namely that while technology is reshaping just about everything, including dealmaking, it's also making human interventions and interactions even more important. In this context, strategy is a fascinating place to start our journey because it relies heavily on the instinct and experience of very senior executives and their often more independent and strategically minded board of directors, usually complemented by forward-thinking external advisers. Strategy can be developed outside of the boardroom but is rarely set outside of it. Once it leaves the boardroom the task is largely to action it, not question it.

This has its advantages because strategy is notoriously difficult to execute and is always at risk of being derailed. So, if it isn't fully owned by those leaders, and actioned by their subordinates, what chance will it have? In addition, strategy often requires just the sort of creative thinking and leaps of faith that only a strong-minded leader can make. The counter-argument is that it's just such individualistic thinking that can lead to disaster and therefore all decisions should instead be based on hard facts and data, especially when they concern billions of dollars and thousands of employees and shareholders. They should also, therefore, be subject to the review of the independent directors.

Kodak/Xerox and Tesla: different sides of the same coin

Famously, Eastman Kodak was the first company to invent the handheld digital camera in 1975 but then failed to build it into their strategy (Gann, 2016). Human instinct and organizational inertia made senior executives, wedded to the photographic film and non-digital cameras that had been their great success since the company's founding in 1892, resist an idea that fundamentally undermined their business model. Kodak filed for bankruptcy in January 2012 (although it emerged from bankruptcy around a year and a half later as a mere shadow of its former industry-leader self and with a focus on traditional non-digital photography) (Djudjic, 2018). It's not just Kodak who ignored new technologies and business models. Ubiquitous photocopier company Xerox famously developed the concepts that underly all our personal computer interfaces (task windows, icons and a hand-controlled mouse with clicker) in the early 1970s, and although they developed what many consider to be the first personal computer, they never commercialized it as management were focused on their traditional business area (Smith and Alexander, 1999). This enabled Steve Jobs to use those concepts in the wildly successful Apple computers (Montag, 2018). One can be sure that Xerox considers the missed opportunity of the PC as 'one that got away'.

It doesn't have to end this way. In contrast in a totally different industry, Tesla had no such baggage and embraced new automotive technology right from the outset. Yet there is one similarity between the two companies in terms of strategy. Tesla's charismatic founder Elon Musk could be said to employ 'gut instinct' just as much as Kodak's or Xerox's researchers. Instead of, as is common in tech firms, producing a low-cost, minimum viable product that would keep initial costs down, Tesla made a luxurious, expensive, fully featured sports car right from the start to allow for tweaking and creating future economies of scale. By turning previous thinking upside down, Elon Musk had something exciting to show investors and, crucially, produced cars that created a brand-building buzz. By 2020, only 17 years after being founded, Tesla was worth more than the rest of the biggest companies in the automobile industry put together (Ausick, 2020).

Behavioural factors

What these three examples neatly illustrate is the tendency for strategy, and we believe therefore any M&A deals used to enact it, to be about big bets based on gut instinct. Given this context, it's perhaps surprising that human behavioural factors have been often ignored in studies of strategy and M&A. Even more so, given the dreadful success rate of M&A deals which historically was no greater than 20–40 per cent, although today can at best claim a 50 per cent success rate, based on our analyses at Bayes Business School over the past 15 to 20 years (Moeller and Brady, 2014) that we also mentioned in the previous chapter. And this success rate is remarkably consistent across the various measurements of success, whether it's an increase in shareholder value, market share or profitability or other non-financial factors such as a reduction in employee turnover or the number of patents issued to the company.

Additionally, studies show that companies who are active in the M&A markets outperform those who don't do any deals, especially in the period after the appointment of a new CEO (Appadu et al, 2016). A note of caution must be struck, however, about the value of doing multiple deals over a short period of time as the process of post-deal integration can be very demanding and distracting to the core business. So, far from boosting performance, doing too many deals too quickly can actually, over time, lead to a decrease in returns for the acquirer.

That said, a 50 per cent success rate is still not good enough as it's no better than a coin flip. Should boards be approving tens of thousands of acquisitions annually when the historical evidence of success is so poor? This is even more surprising as so many executives still believe the 'old' historical data and prevailing conventional wisdom showing that up to 80 per cent of M&A deals fail.

In the absence of a broad range of studies that directly link M&A with human behaviours, we must turn instead to the broader field of behavioural finance, which can be traced right back to economist Adam Smith's work in the 18th century and his treatise on the 'invisible hand of the market' (Smith, 2010). Since then, modern studies have brought us now-familiar terms such as loss aversion (Tversky and Kahneman, 1991) and irrational exuberance (Schiller, 2016), as well as unearthing a host of other psychological factors that can all distort financial judgement (Moeller, 2022).

Some of these are particularly relevant and even specific to M&A. Perhaps the most relevant one here is Richard Roll's 1986 study of managerial overconfidence and optimism (the so-called 'hubris hypothesis') (Roll, 1986). It is this factor that causes boards to approve deals despite the historical evidence, believing that they have the magic sauce for success or that 'this time it will be different'.

Distilling this and other studies since, let's briefly examine the psychological biases and heuristics that affect both strategy and deal-making, then move on to how the new capabilities provided by, for example, big data collection and analysis can negate, balance or even enhance these natural tendencies.

BEHAVIOURAL BIASES AFFECTING M&A DEALS

Although not an exhaustive list, the following biases are those most often observed in M&A deals and featured in 'A study of how behavioural finance theory applies to the senior management decision-making process in M&A' (Moeller, 2022):

Overconfidence/excessive optimism

People make mistakes more frequently when they believe themselves to be better than average, also overestimating how frequently they will experience favourable outcomes. This has added relevance here if we assume, quite safely as most readers would probably agree, that those who set strategies and do deals are unlikely to have risen to such a role without having been successful in business and holding a strong belief in themselves and their judgement.

Confirmation bias

This bias occurs when people attach too much importance to information that supports their views rather than that which runs counter to those views. A victim of such bias tends to notice and seek information that confirms preconceptions and ignores or discounts anything that contradicts those initial beliefs.

Illusion of control

When people overestimate the extent to which they can control events, they tend to ignore external factors that can have an impact on their decisions. The risk is that a strategy based on such an illusion will not be practical as soon as it leaves the boardroom.

Information availability bias

This is when a decision maker relies too heavily on knowledge that is readily available, rather than examining information that is more difficult to obtain. In terms of both strategy and M&A, the danger is favouring what and who the CEO knows and disregarding potentially better options that are less familiar.

Affect heuristic

Put simply, this describes basing decisions primarily on intuition, instinct and gut feeling. Put another way, it's the reason why some people buy damp, difficult to heat and hard to maintain houses they have fallen in love with, rather than choose perfectly insulated and fully equipped houses that just don't give them the same positive emotional feeling.

> Hubris hypothesis
>
> The hubris hypothesis, mentioned earlier, goes beyond confirmation bias and incorporates the idea that the individual, usually the leader of an organization, believes that they can do no wrong. Within the M&A arena, it is manifested by dealmakers and CEOs who have done one or more successful deals and believe their own public relations (and the 'yes' people who surround them) who say that any deal they touch will naturally, and perhaps with little extra effort, be successful.
>
> These factors do not exist in isolation. They often combine, as, for example, overconfidence in making an acquisition can be a result of information availability bias and the affect heuristic. To use our earlier analogy, why does a buyer who has fallen in love with a house still go through with the purchase despite finding significant rising damp in the basement? Perhaps because they had a previous house where they were able to fix a similar problem, ignoring the fact that no two houses, or indeed rising damp problems, are identical.

The dangerous human

Given the vital importance of dealmaking in our ever more rapidly changing world, our brief foray into human behavioural factors gives us plenty of cause for concern. Can such momentous decisions really be left to humans with fragile egos and sometimes questionable decision-making skills? Let's look now at how technology is providing the equivalent of a cold shower and a chance for cool, calm reflection.

The use of new technology in setting strategies

This book isn't the place to go into great detail on the workings of these new technologies, so we will focus instead on their outcomes and impact. In doing so we assume that readers will broadly understand the ability of technology to scour not only existing databases but also to gather structured and unstructured data from text, video and audio sources, and how this is taking machine learning and AI capabilities to new levels, powered by algorithms and bots capable of scraping and analysing literally millions of pieces of information in milliseconds.

Focusing on outcomes, these innovative new technologies have three main ways to add value in relation to strategy:

1 First, by helping companies to analyse huge amounts of data and information in business-critical areas such as market conditions, customer behaviours and complex global supply chains. What's more, instead of capturing a single snapshot, technology, including AI, enables firms to constantly monitor such areas in real time. For example, we'll hear from Steve King, the CEO of Black Swan Data, in Chapter 2 about how his AI-driven tools are turning social media chat into actionable insights. Products and technologies like this can assist decision making by making sure that even the most gut- and instinct-driven senior executives start from a sound basis and are able to test their strategies against the facts and data about current realities. Tools have also been developed which provide rich insights as to where your competitors – both traditional and emerging – are investing, giving users a more holistic view of where the market is moving. This transparency is helping boardrooms to see that standing still is no longer enough and therefore encourages strategic change. New technological tools also provide the opportunity to explore a redefinition of the market, its implications, and the opportunities of what would otherwise not be recognized or identified without applying these new technologies. Through the use of data heat maps, for example, one can more easily visualize the changes over time between sectors, regions and even at country and company level. These tools make information accessible for boards and senior executives who otherwise may not have the time to dig into the depths of the data available, therefore boosting their strategic decision making.

2 Second, with the data just described, alternative strategies can be modelled, tested and, where necessary, adjusted. We will come back to that scenario testing in a moment with relation to M&A,

but the key point here is that technology is helping decision makers to consider their options more fully.

3 Third, and the area that is perhaps the most exciting, by identifying trends and patterns in data, technologies such as AI can create and then plot future scenarios and predict possible if not even likely outcomes. This gives machines the potential to go beyond providing the insights and automation described so far. By analysing ever greater and broader datasets, technology-driven tools can identify market opportunities and suggest different business strategies to take advantage of them, taking into account, for example, estimated entry costs and risks under different market conditions over different timeframes. Just as importantly, there's no need to rely on a single or even just a few scenarios on which to base the strategy and related acquisitions, as computing power will allow for an almost unlimited number of alternatives. Similarly, the new technologies enable each of those myriad scenarios within each alternative strategy to be properly and thoroughly stress tested, with a selection then made for those most likely to occur.

It's clear that to support this strategy, the same data and technology could also be used to analyse the risks and opportunities involved in doing deals. The respective merits of using organic growth, joint venture, business partnership, merger or acquisition to advance strategy could all be assessed. For example, in a potential business partnership, this would mean looking at the levels of market competition, the similarities and differences of products offered, the elasticity of prices, the pools of human talent, various supply chain options and the potential gains arising from an exchange of technology and business know-how.

While this information will not replace the human need to build the personal relationships essential to most business partnerships, it is likely to provide more solid foundations for those partnerships – and perhaps help to spare us from investing time in partnerships that are not aligned to the desired strategic outcome.

Does opportunity eat strategy for breakfast?

Eagle-eyed readers and real-life dealmakers will have already spotted a fatal flaw to this technology-enabled virtual utopia. No matter how many green lights are flashing on the virtual tech-driven dashboard, deals are very often driven by opportunity rather than strategy. If a key competitor or supplier puts up the 'for sale' sign, for example, it can quickly become a great idea to buy the company, even if it was never anticipated in your strategy.

COMBINING OPPORTUNITY AND STRATEGY IN DEALMAKING

To examine this further, let's take you back to the 1990s when one of our authors was working for a multinational banking company, which had identified a chink in its strategic armour. With a large and successful commercial banking operation spanning the globe and a strong retail position in Europe, the bank decided that the one missing piece of the jigsaw was a similarly strong global investment banking operation, despite an acquisition made in this area a decade earlier, with a particular need for scale in the United States.

Beefing up that nascent investment banking arm organically would take far too long in a world built on teams and relationships that need time to grow and develop. Hostile takeovers were judged as being too risky in the banking sector (and RBS's acquisition of ABN Amro almost a decade later proved this assumption to be correct) (Pratley, 2011). Joint ventures or partnerships were unlikely to find favour, so our author was charged with coming up with a hybrid dealmaking approach that encompassed both the strategic and opportunistic. This involved keeping and updating files on a large number of potential targets, so that when one did pop up on the horizon, the gun was loaded to bag the opportunity.

It's not hard to see how the technology detailed earlier could not only replace our diligent colleague's word processor notes and the analytical abilities of three or four equally diligent analysts using spreadsheets in Lotus 1-2-3 (a precursor spreadsheet program that might not be as old as Visicalc, but predated Microsoft's Excel), but could add much more, with AI

> bots constantly scouring sources to keep an updated 'war file' on each potential acquisition. With their ability to mine text and spoken word, AI programs might even be able to better predict when targets could be most susceptible to a bid.
>
> The end to that story, however, provides an interesting insight. The news that an overseas rival might be willing to combine forces or even sell up came, not from AI or the rigorous analytical efforts of the internal corporate development team, but through a casual and opportunistic chat between two senior banking executives. That's a tough call for even the most sophisticated technology to replicate.

Yet one more factor that technology can't replicate is the need to develop a trusting relationship between the two negotiating parties. This trusting relationship needs to be not just between the principals in the negotiation, but also the advisers who will often play a critical role in many parts of the dealmaking process. Deals ultimately get done because there is trust built between the buyer and the seller. Trust that the buyer will stick to their promises in the deal-closing agreements, trust that employees will be taken care of, and trust that the two businesses can continue to collaborate throughout the Transition Services Agreement (TSA) period, for example. This will be a major theme of Chapter 3 on *Winning hearts, minds and money*, but relates to the strategy development stage of the deal as well.

There's been a lot of discussion so far in this chapter on the technology and human factors that drive strategy, including where they overlap and even complement each other. Let's extract the key points:

- This is a world where humans make the big calls because, essentially, that's what they're hired and paid to do.
- With the necessity that trust must exist between both parties to the M&A deal, it's only amongst humans that such trust can be developed.
- Although in-built human failings can prove expensive, they can also be outweighed by the many positives that come with our ability to think laterally and creatively.

- The serendipity of human conversations and interactions will still result in some opportunistic deals that no search of big data nor application of AI will ever be able to identify (as with our example of the cross-border banking deal discussed above).
- So, humans are very much here to stay at the centre of strategy – but data and technology will play an ever-greater role in providing them with a better base for decision making and for building the platform on which trust can be built.
- And lastly, once that 'better' strategy is selected, the implementation should be more confident and perhaps, if appropriate, quicker as there was extensive and robust data and analysis supporting the strategy.

It's a win-win situation in which human blind spots are minimized by technology but the ultimate responsibility still rests with those who must commit to and enact the strategy within an organization. In popular terms, relating this to the original *Star Trek* television series, every Captain James T. Kirk needs a logical Science Officer Spock (but both still need a powerful onboard computer).

From theory to practice: strategy in action

Now let's move on to the undoubted star of this chapter, Robert Lawson. He's a man who, despite his fresh-faced appearance and youthful energy, has spent over 30 years at energy giant BP, including the last decade as global head of M&A. That not only places him at the very heart of the action as BP starts to deliver on its net zero ambition, it also puts him in a great position to help us further explore the issues raised so far in this chapter.

Strategies develop over time

BP's corporate website positions its current transformation as being just one stage in a long journey that traces back to the company's founding over a century ago in 1909: 'Our story has always been about transitions – from coal to oil, from oil to gas, from onshore to deep water and now onwards towards a new mix of energy sources as the world moves into a lower-carbon future' (BP, 2022).

However, there are a couple of major differences that are worthy of closer examination in the context of our book.

First, let's examine what kicked off this big strategic shift. Climate change has, after all, been on the horizon and agenda for many years. As far back as 1997, their hugely respected CEO John Browne made a highly publicized speech about the need to reduce carbon emissions and the steps BP would take to do so (Castillo, 1997). Of course, public and government pressure on climate change has intensified massively since that speech, but Rob believes that the 2020 appointment of BP CEO Bernard Looney provided fresh impetus to tackle this huge challenge. As Rob puts it, 'A new chief exec was able to launch a new and bold strategy and use the moment to engage with multiple stakeholders.' So, even though the pressure for such a seismic and strategic transition had been emerging through time, it takes acts of leadership to make that call and get it moving.

Second, we can see first-hand how the disruptive factors we talked about earlier in the chapter – from new technologies to sustainability – directly impact both BP's strategy and the way that plays out in terms of M&A. Essentially, that level of disruption makes the strategic change to be both greater and less linear. As Rob puts it, 'We've had transformations before but this one has touched every single part of the organization. Previously what we had were two segments: upstream and downstream. In 2020 we reinvented and rewired the whole organization in order to deliver the new strategy.' While Rob explains that analysis and modelling played an important role in developing the strategy, he also recognizes that such a seismic shift requires the human ability to communicate with and win over a wide range of stakeholders including board members, investors, staff and NGOs (non-governmental organizations), a topic we return to in Chapter 6.

The deal on deals

Those complexities around strategy have translated into a more complex deal landscape. Rob continues: 'As we become an integrated energy company there are more operating businesses and the need for more joint ventures lines, including solar, hydrogen, biofuels, electric vehicle charging, as well as oil and gas.

'The role of our M&A team is changing as a result of that transition. We're divesting assets at different parts of their life cycle, often with different levels of carbon within the assets. Then we're also tasked with buying, much more than historically, smaller companies and more nascent companies with early track records and emerging technologies.'

This is how M&A supports the strategy of a company: divesting assets that are no longer necessary to the long-term strategy (their sale is another company's acquisition) and then filling in the necessary new elements of that strategy with the purchase (acquisition) of new businesses.

DEALS THAT SUPPORT STRATEGY

Rob agrees that strategy must drive M&A, not vice-versa, and chose two examples to illustrate the point:

- In 2018, BP acquired the UK's largest electric vehicle (EV) charging network, Chargemaster, for £130 million (BBC, 2018). And in 2021, BP added to its capabilities in this field with the purchase of US-based fleet charging start-up Amply (Hurst and Baker, 2021).

    Strategic rationale: investment in fast, convenient EV charging is key to helping customers reduce emissions and meet changing customer demand as consumers have started buying electric vehicles to replace their internal combustion automobiles. The acquisition leverages BP's brand as a supplier of fuel and owner of petrol stations, while maintaining its relevance for customers in an increasingly electric future.

- In 2020, BP entered the offshore wind market through a $1.1 billion partnership with US energy firm Equinor to develop US East Coast offshore wind projects and jointly seek other opportunities in the fast-growing US wind farm market (Ambrose, 2020).

    Strategic rationale: this represented BP's first offshore wind venture and an important step towards its aim of having developed 50 gigawatts of renewable power by 2030. It also leverages BP's decades of experience

> of operating offshore with its massive oil rigs in hostile weather and ocean conditions, which can act as a competitive advantage in the offshore wind market.
>
> We should stress that these are just two examples: BP has been busy on the M&A front across the globe, from taking stakes in early-stage companies with exciting new technologies to divesting multibillion-dollar oil and gas assets.

New technologies, new skills

We've seen how disruptive forces are shaking up strategy and taking even the biggest global companies like BP into unchartered territory. So, if there was ever a case where deal technology could provide support and add value to dealmaking, this may well be it.

What does Rob think? 'Clearly our ability to look at data, gather insights and analyse situations is increasing year-on-year, with better tools and better data, but is there a magic button that tells us if we should be in this market or that market? I don't believe there is. Ultimately it boils down to people in a room forming a view from the data in front of them as to what works for us and what works for our stakeholders.'

If that sounds like Rob is in any way diminishing the role of technology, then think again. From using Microsoft's Power BI to create interactive dashboards to data visualizations of the current and future EV charging market, he is a keen adopter of available technologies. But rather than seeing them as a replacement for the human aspects of dealmaking, he sees them as an augmentation.

'Technology enables human decisions to be made more effectively,' he explains.

So, for example, although Rob hired the best people to advise him on the EV market, used advanced software to model outcomes and indicate deal prices, ultimately 'the deal valuation is what the owner is willing to sell at and so inevitably it becomes about negotiation, about connecting across the table and trying to find deal space.'

He adds: 'Speaking to employees in the target company and getting a view on their capabilities will remain vital. Not least because when we buy into companies, we are looking to work with the management team, not to replace them. Ultimately, we want the right people with the right attitude, who will interface with the broader BP. The human element is really important.'

What remote working told us about humans and technology

During the first UK lockdown in 2020, Rob was responsible for overseeing the $5 billion (£4.1 billion) sale of BP's chemicals business to INEOS entirely from the comfort of his home office (BP, 2020). That might seem to present an extremely powerful case for the triumph of technology, but Rob feels that it was only possible because the two companies had transacted before: 'We knew the counterparty and had a very good, constructive relationship with our opposite numbers in the deal process, so a level of trust was already there.' In contrast, 'where we haven't known the counterparty, doing deals remotely has been very challenging.'

That suggests that while technology can do much to support strategy and dealmaking, people will remain at the core. 'I don't think M&A dealmaking is a process that is succumbing to robots and I don't think human beings risk disintermediation from it,' explains Rob.

That influences his view of the future. Despite welcoming the next generation of software, data science and AI to support and improve the deal process, he believes change will be incremental, not seismic. 'I don't think it's an either/or situation – it's the interplay of the two,' he adds.

There is one exception, however. He explains, 'I think in five to ten years' time you're still going to need people with a track record of trust who can build relationships, but you may not need as many lawyers, given that legal and contractual documentation has the potential for much greater automation.'

In other words, it is the core elements of human input that will endure because they remain crucial in setting and selling strategy, then carrying out the resulting deals. But anything outside those core human elements, from analysts to lawyers, may be made more effective and efficient by technology or even entirely replaced by it.

Stay in your lane: how bad habits get checked

Remember how earlier in this chapter we explored the flip side to the human qualities we have just cited as so essential and everlasting? Those were the human behavioural biases that can run havoc, unleashing egos and half-baked analyses that risk driving through unsuitable deals and are blind to better judgement.

Rob has an interesting angle on this, stressing how such dangers can be addressed through good governance. For example, he explains how his M&A team are kept independent of the broader business and that there are also a number of checks and balances in place before a deal can be signed off. These range from high-level investment committees to board approvals to the role that the internal legal department, human resources (HR) and other specialists within BP play in scrutinizing the relevant aspects of deals.

This also impacts another area highlighted earlier in this chapter, namely the opportunistic deals that are driven less by strategy and more by the fact that the companies put themselves up for sale. Rob believes that, with the level of independence and oversight in place, that is unlikely to happen. 'The chance of a big, well-governed organization like ours jumping on a deal that wasn't on the radar but suddenly becomes available is slim,' he says.

In explaining why that is the case, Rob provides perhaps the perfect summary, warning and indeed closing line for this chapter: 'Everything we in the M&A team do has to be in service of the pre-agreed strategy.'

> **KEY POINTS**
>
> - Market disruption from technology is requiring fundamental changes in strategy.
>
> - Deals enable companies to deliver on their strategy more quickly than organic growth.
>
> - Technology is helping companies to set and test strategy, but, especially with the importance of trust to the deal completion process, business leaders will always be the final decision makers and implementers of that strategy.

References

Ambrose, J (2020) Global oil demand may have passed peak, *The Guardian*, 14 September, www.theguardian.com/business/2020/sep/14/global-oil-demand-may-have-passed-peak-says-bp-energy-report (archived at https://perma.cc/48KS-WR47)

Appadu, N, Carapeto, M, Faelten, A, Moeller, S and Vitkova, V (2016) What should I do next? CEO succession and subsequent M&A strategy, SSRN, https://ssrn.com/abstract=4278687 (archived at https://perma.cc/G8N6-MZ6E)

Ausick, P (2020) Tesla is worth more than all big car companies in the world combined, *24/7 Wall St.*, 22 December, https://247wallst.com/autos/2020/12/22/tesla-is-worth-more-than-all-big-car-companies-in-the-world-combined/ (archived at https://perma.cc/MHR6-NSV9)

BBC (2018) BP buys UK's largest car charging firm Chargemaster, *BBC News*, 28 June, www.bbc.co.uk/news/business-44640647 (archived at https://perma.cc/3CKC-CPMN)

BP (2020) BP agrees to sell its petrochemicals business to INEOS, 29 June, www.BP.com/en/global/corporate/news-and-insights/press-releases/BP-agrees-to-sell-its-petrochemicals-business-to-ineos.html (archived at https://perma.cc/9UMU-KW2Y)

BP (no date) Our history, www.BP.com/en/global/corporate/who-we-are/our-history.html (archived at https://perma.cc/MD9M-JJ92)

Carapeto, M, Moeller, S and Faelten, A (2010) What should I do next? CEO succession and subsequent M&A strategy, Mergers and Acquisitions Research Centre, Bayes Business School, 15 January

Castillo, C (1997) British Petroleum CEO Browne says firm will respond on global warming, *Stanford Report*, 21 May, https://news.stanford.edu/news/1997/may21/bp.html (archived at https://perma.cc/UA6R-6SPG)

Chen, B X (2014) Apple to pay $3 billion to buy Beats, *The New York Times*, 28 May, www.nytimes.com/2014/05/29/technology/apple-confirms-its-3-billion-deal-for-beats-electronics.html (archived at https://perma.cc/KR6E-8AQV)

Djudjic, D (2018) From photo industry giant to bankruptcy: what happened to Kodak? *DIY Photography*, 15 June, www.diyphotography.net/from-photo-industry-giant-to-bankruptcy-what-happened-to-kodak/ (archived at https://perma.cc/RU86-4EJ5)

Espósito, F (2022) Apple leads the headphone market in the US with Airpods and Beats, *9to5Mac*, 10 February, https://9to5mac.com/2022/02/10/apple-leads-the-headphone-market-in-the-us-with-airpods-and-beats/ (archived at https://perma.cc/W9CD-3YXR)

Gann, D (2016) Kodak invented the digital camera – then killed it. Why innovation often fails, *World Economic Forum*, 23 June, www.weforum.org/agenda/2016/06/leading-innovation-through-the-chicanes/ (archived at https://perma.cc/XG34-QQEG)

Hurst, L and Baker, D R (2021) BP expands EV charging business in U.S. with Amply power deal, *Bloomberg UK*, 7 December, www.bloomberg.com/news/articles/2021-12-07/bp-expands-ev-charging-business-in-u-s-with-amply-power-deal (archived at https://perma.cc/3AMJ-42JT)

Marino, J (2015) Goldman Sachs is a tech company, *Business Insider*, 12 April, www.businessinsider.in/finance/goldman-sachs-is-a-tech-company/articleshow/46897984.cms (archived at https://perma.cc/CH3S-7QXH)

Moeller, S (2022) A study of how behavioural finance theory applies to the senior management decision-making process in M&A Bayes Business School, https://papers.ssrn.com/sol3/papers.cfm?abstract_id=4043808 (archived at https://perma.cc/XK4N-TXWZ)

Moeller, S and Brady, C (2014) *Intelligent M&A: Navigating the mergers and acquisitions minefield* (2nd edition), John Wiley and Sons, Chichester

Montag, S (2018) Why your computer has a mouse according to Steve Jobs in 1985, *CNBC*, 21 May, www.cnbc.com/2018/05/21/why-your-computer-has-a-mouse-according-to-steve-jobs.html (archived at https://perma.cc/TZ96-MFMM)

Peyton, A (2018) Goldman Sachs acquires financial modelling firm ClearFactr, *FinTech Futures*, 12 November, www.fintechfutures.com/2018/11/goldman-sachs-acquires-financial-modelling-firm-clearfactr/ (archived at https://perma.cc/4VK5-EQ46)

Pratley, N (2011) What was RBS board thinking when it backed ABN Amro takeover? It wasn't, *The Guardian*, 12 December, www.theguardian.com/business/nils-pratley-on-finance/2011/dec/12/what-rbs-board-thinking-abn-amro (archived at https://perma.cc/T39A-D4BB)

Roll, R (1986) The hubris hypothesis of corporate takeovers, *The Journal of Business*, **59** (2), pp 197–216 (April)

Schiller, R (2016) *Irrational Exuberance*, 3rd ed, Princeton University Press, Princeton and Oxford

Smith, A (2010, [1759]) *The Theory of Moral Sentiments*, A. Millar, Edinburgh

Smith, D and Alexander, R (1999) *Fumbling the Future*, ToExcel, Lincoln, NE

Sohail, O (2021) Apple has sold 2 billion iPhones, silencing critics and keeping jobs' legacy alive, *Wccftech*, 22 September, https://wccftech.com/apple-has-sold-2-billion-iphones/ (archived at https://perma.cc/ED3V-TXBV)

Tversky, A and Kahneman, D (1991) Loss aversion in riskless choice: A reference-dependent model, *The Quarterly Journal of Economics*, www.jstor.org/stable/2937956 (archived at https://perma.cc/Y53J-3ZP7)

2

Identify your target

*From sitting ducks to moving goalposts:
why finding the right target has got tougher
and how technology is helping out*

In Chapter 1 we described how, back in the pre-millennium past, one of our authors worked for a global bank that was looking to beef up its investment banking operations by making an acquisition. Given the limited range of potential targets – essentially, other major banks that might be willing to divest their investment banking operations or smaller boutique banks that could be swallowed whole – our author's job was relatively simple and straightforward: maintain comprehensive and up-to-date information on those potential targets so that, should one come to market, the business would be prepared.

It was an effective strategy but one that could be compared to an old-fashioned funfair shooting game. The rifle is ready and primed; it's just a question of waiting until the target pops up and then the trigger can be pulled, perhaps preceded by a little judicious stalking of the prey to help it break cover and put itself firmly in the acquirer's sights.

While that strategy remains effective for some companies, it does not reflect the changing realities for many as they increasingly look to acquire as a route to growth/market, or indeed survival, in today's fast-changing, shape-shifting markets.

That's because, as the volume and pace of disruption increases, it is fragmenting sectors, blurring their boundaries, converging industries (for example, is Amazon a technology company or a retailer – or both?) and opening up previously 'moated' markets or industry capabilities to new players.

For example, big banks that once acquired companies strictly within their own financial services sector boundaries have, since the digital age dawned, been busy buying tech companies to help them transition to online banking and beyond. Increasingly, they are also facing new competition from digital-only financial service providers who are resetting customer expectations, which the current incumbents must now match or exceed.

While automotive manufacturers, to use another example, have always had large and complex supply chains which they tightly controlled in order to assure consistent, timely and efficient production, they now find themselves increasingly reliant on powerful chip manufacturers and battery producers as the automotive industry electrifies and many car components rely more and more on technology. These pressures are not only opening up the market to dynamic new players like Tesla, they are also rapidly changing usage and vehicle ownership models, which in turn need new technology, operating models and financing capabilities to support them.

These requirements could be developed from scratch within those traditional automotive manufacturers, but that may take too long as the pace of change outstrips their ability to hire, train and retain employees who not only have the requisite skills but the strategic insight to use them effectively and efficiently. So, the alternative is to acquire those skills by purchasing another company that has already carried out the hiring, training and strategizing. These acquisitions would typically have an organizational and operational structure already in place, not only to retain these employees but also to harness their ability to continue developing new products.

No going back: the multi-dimensional, moving target range

The examples are near endless as sector after sector finds the ground shifting beneath its very feet. Clearly, keeping up in this kind of market is hard to do, so acquisitions, as noted earlier, remain attractive as a 'shortcut' to sustaining market relevance and accessing growth, but the days in which finding targets is simply a matter of waiting for the right target to pop up are largely gone. Today, targets are not only moving but are also multi-dimensional: more like a cutting-edge, multi-layered computer game than the old-school funfair shooting game described previously. Rob Lawson, former global head of M&A at BP, who featured in Chapter 1, neatly summed up this new perspective: 'The role of our M&A team is changing... we're divesting assets at different parts of their life cycle... we're also tasked with buying, much more than historically, smaller companies and more nascent companies with early track records and emerging technologies.'

It's worth noting that these changes are having an impact on digital value and that goes well beyond how targets are identified. As we will discuss in Chapter 7, it is also impacting integration, with greater significance now being put on realizing technological synergies and understanding its implications on the new (combined) organization. Instead of traditional integration, which would have been more focused on quickly finding areas of 'rationalization', there is a greater need for the human and technological talents and capabilities of the acquired company to not only be kept but flourish in a post-deal environment.

A new dimension in dealmaking

So rapid are the changes taking place, that in many cases acquiring a fully mature business that 'owns' a chunk of the market is now either impossible or risks being a backward-looking deal as such organizations are often legacy companies. So, just as the targets are broadening, so do the deal types, early-stage companies (so-called 'acquisition programmes', 'bolt-on' or 'roll-ups'), joint ventures with technology companies or teaming up with other complementary players in what is becoming commonly referred to as the 'ecosystem'.

That's not our favourite word because of its tendency to mean different things to different people, but it does reflect the fact that, for many corporations, succeeding in today's markets means operating across sectors, supply chains, platforms and technologies. Owning that whole ecosystem is, for all but the very biggest and most vertically integrated companies, largely out of the question but choosing the right parts and people to engage with is crucial. And interestingly that often means cooperating as well as competing.

We will look at an example of one such ecosystem shortly, but the immediate problem is crystal clear. Given this greater complexity, how can companies – which, after all, have plenty else to keep them busy at present – identify the targets that will help them advance their strategy?

The perfect environment for technology

Fortunately, this is an area where technology has a key role to play and indeed is already fulfilling it, leveraging its ability to not only slice and dice data but understand acquirers' needs and model future growth spots. We will go on to examine and list those technologies in more detail in this chapter and talk to a leading player, whose responsibilities include overseeing the creation of a powerful platform that helps companies to see the whole picture as they seek to find the right targets. We will also be talking to a partner at the globally renowned SoftBank Vision Fund about the relationship between technology and human insight when it comes to identifying and assessing targets.

First, let's summarize the range of challenges facing companies seeking to use deals as a strategic tool. Some of these we have already highlighted, while others are getting their first airing here:

- more choice of targets because of the need to operate across sectors, capabilities and ecosystems;
- pressure to acquire companies at earlier stages of development rather than waiting for the winners to emerge;
- increasing need for acquirers to step out of their 'comfort zone' beyond their home markets, core products and services and capabilities;

- the need to respond to rapid changes in consumer behaviour, need and expectation.

Underlying all of the above is the now-continual demand for companies to up their games across a range of areas, from technology to sustainability and inclusion, specifically:

- Pressure to acquire technology capabilities, both in the production and operations of the core (and future core) businesses, but also in response to the technology demands of customers whose communication tool of choice is ever changing.
- Demand to adapt the entire company and its products and services to a world that needs to be more focused on climate and the environment. This is driving companies to develop new capabilities, for example PepsiCo striking up a partnership with plant-based food company Beyond Meat in 2021 to develop a range of snacks and beverages made from plant-based protein (Matthews, 2021).
- The imperative to make sure that the company's culture is inclusive and equitable and that its products, services, marketing, distribution and indeed all aspects of the firm's operations reflect this.

ESG as a deal driver

The role of dealmaking in helping companies become more environmentally friendly and inclusive can be seen in a recent study by Bayes Business School (Huang et al, 2022). It showed, for example, that companies acquiring another company with a higher environmental, social and governance (ESG) rating are more likely to improve their own rating. Indeed, the study showed that companies are actively using acquisitions as a tool to improve their ESG performance.

Taking a step back and looking at ESG more broadly, we have seen how, over the last few years, it has reshaped the relationship between corporates and investors, as well as the investment philosophy of many global financial players.

As a result, those companies and M&A dealmakers that adopt long-term ESG objectives are likely to attract additional capital at more favourable conditions. Having said this, there is a perception amongst the public and investors that so-called 'greenwashing' is prevalent. In response, companies and private equity (PE) funds are now constantly tracking and monitoring the ESG data of their targets to make sure it aligns with their own long-term sustainability objectives, while also expecting deal advisers to do the same.

With the rise of ESG matters firmly on the executive agenda, we expect that ESG-driven motives will generate a sizeable level of M&A activity in the future, particularly where firms are planning to improve their ecological and climate footprint and therefore consider purchasing, rationalizing and/or divesting their asset portfolio. So, as well as adding another filter to apply when looking for targets, there is – given the lack of universally accepted, standardized ESG standards – the added uncertainty over which metrics to use when applying that filter.

Taking your vitamins: finding targets in a fragmented marketplace

To further illustrate the current complexity facing companies in identifying targets, let's look at the global consumer goods companies wishing to exploit opportunities in the fast-growing nutritional supplements sub-sector. To clarify, this sub-sector features non-prescription vitamin-type supplements that are targeted at individuals who may be looking, for example, to boost their sports performance, optimize their health or improve general wellbeing.

This is an attractive growth area for consumer goods companies because it plays into the growing theme of 'health and wellbeing' and provides them with an opportunity to leverage their marketing and product development strengths. At first glance, readers may think that pharma companies would already hold an advantageous position in this market because they effectively hold the keys to the medicine cabinet. However, because nutritional supplements are often non-prescription and generally not highly regulated, the market is open to consumer goods companies in a way that many other health-related markets are not. But that very openness also means that there are many smaller players all along the value chain, including diagnostics firms who help consumers decide what products they need, small-scale manufacturers, niche online retailers, as well as non-traditional physical retailers including gyms and health centres.

As any runner, gym-goer, swimmer, yoga fan or keen walker will know, it's also a marketplace where trends are constantly changing and new ideas and products are continually appearing and, just as rapidly, going out of fashion or favour.

For large consumer goods companies, which might traditionally focus investment on major food, beauty and homecare brands with long, complex product development processes, these types of market dynamics can be a daunting prospect as well as a great opportunity to leverage their existing strengths. The first stage of the process is to really understand all the moving parts in the value chain and what types of companies are operating in this specific sub-sector.

Instead of spending time on undertaking these analyses manually there are now technologies and search engines/platforms that can crunch a huge amount of data and slice and dice it to identify the areas where the potential acquirer wants to dive into more detail. This not only saves time, it can also unearth companies that the acquirer may not otherwise have been able to source and identify. And in addition, the whole value chain analysis that such tools can deliver provides valuable insight into the best segments to enter.

After such detailed assessment of the value chain, its components and the companies operating within it, the acquirer will be able to better identify where within that value chain they want to add capabilities, whether that be building on their existing position or creating new ones. Even for a major consumer goods company, developing a position from scratch in such a niche and fast-moving market may not be the best strategy, and buying their way into existing players and platforms may make more sense. That is typically done through joint ventures and stake building in promising start-ups. Here, the ability of such search engines/platforms to identify even the smallest players right across the ecosystem is highly valuable. This can often be supplemented with information on where the 'hot money' is flowing, provided by tracking the amount of investment already attracted by individual companies and sub-sectors.

Technology to the rescue: platforms are smarter than people

So, if we can take one thing from this chapter so far, it's that this is a challenge perfectly set up for technology to ride to the rescue by collating information, analysing the marketplace and identifying targets. That's important because of the sheer volume of data available on companies and transactions. For example, one platform that helps potential acquirers to identify targets offers access to over 90,000 publicly-listed companies, 10.4 million private companies, and 4 million start-ups, as well as holding details of over 2.2 million transactions from the past 20 years – and that's in addition to all the structured and unstructured public and private company data sets it holds, supplied by leading sources such as Bloomberg, Reuters, Intralinks and the like.

Before we go on to examine the variety of platforms that enable such analysis, it's worth sharing the authors' anecdotal evidence that the sort of information just described can often be a revelation to large legacy players in sectors like consumer goods. The sheer speed with which small companies can set themselves up, then use their online marketing and e-commerce skills to find an audience and scale up, means that sometimes the first corporates know of these rivals and potential targets is when such a rigorous scoping exercise is conducted. That suggests technology has a powerful role in extending the knowledge and ability of even those with many years of sector experience to draw on.

But it would be a mistake to think that it is only the slower-moving and more traditional industries that need help to navigate changing markets to identify targets. In the technology sector, a disproportionate amount of venture capital money, often fuelled by entrepreneurs who have already exited their businesses at high valuations, plus a constant demand for newer and more efficient business to business (B2B) and business to consumer (B2C), means that new tech start-ups have mushroomed across the globe. Instead of the old model, which would have seen tech start-ups exit to larger technology players, the buyer landscape has changed dramatically. More non-technology companies are looking to nascent tech companies to source capabilities and innovation that are difficult or slow for them to build themselves. This is a challenge that takes acquirers out of their comfort zone and, faced with a huge number of options and uncertainties, in need of data-driven insight.

> ### TYPES OF TECHNOLOGY PLATFORMS
>
> Algorithm matching
>
> There are platforms using algorithms to help investors match their requirements to find potential targets. For example, deal platforms such as Axial use their private network to provide sellers with a list of recommended buyers and guide investors who are looking for deals based on pre-determined criteria. Their proprietary algorithm makes matches based on a defined and prioritized list of criteria. Similar platforms of this type currently include Dealsuite, DealNexus, Navatar and SourceScrub, with others being developed all the time.
>
> Multi-model
>
> Other platforms use multiple models to look more broadly across both structured and unstructured data to help companies find buyers or acquirers find targets.
>
> For example, current platforms such as Grata use technologies such as advanced NLP and machine learning to read and structure business information from company websites at scale, providing additional contextual insights about private companies.
>
> Asset monitoring
>
> Another type of platform provides a more holistic view of the landscape of potential targets. There are products, for example, that monitor assets based on a buyer's criteria and use technology to provide real-time updates on any movement within the asset. This real-time view helps buyers to take positive action at the right time rather than, for example, be late to the game when valuations are inflated.

Adviser platforms

There are also companies such as professional services firms launching platforms to enable data-driven origination to underpin their advisory services through the deal cycle. EY Embryonic is one such platform, and has a proprietary algorithm scanning through a data engine containing 18 million companies. The platform uses NLP and ML models to tag companies, applying bespoke sector lenses to improve insights, identify growth areas for investment and highlight potential assets of interest.

Private equity platforms

As well as using some of the third-party platforms mentioned here, PE firms are also creating their own platforms to drive deal origination and beyond. For example, global investment organization EQT has developed its own platform, Motherbrain, which combines external data points, company data and 140,000 unique connections uploaded by EQT employees to create insight and identify targets.

Collectively, platforms like these are fundamentally changing the way we identify targets, by giving corporates and their advisers the ability to:

- search and assess targets across a broader geographic, sector and cross-sector level;
- identify start-ups and early-stage high-growth companies that would normally remain under the radar;
- understand the whole ecosystem in which the buyer wishes to operate;
- track the flow of early-stage and other investment into different areas of the market to reveal competitor activity and 'hot spots';
- identify which part of that ecosystem the buyer can most profitably enter and how it can best do so;
- forecast future market growth and even the potential of individual companies operating within a particular market.

Empowering not eliminating human input

But where does all this leave the human attributes that, as we learned in Chapter 1, still play a leading role in setting the strategy that is then so often enacted through dealmaking? Surely this chapter's argument derails our book's central thesis that deal technology, instead of devaluing human attributes, actually strengthens those human elements and makes them more, not less, important?

The answer is best illustrated through an analogy with modern-day house hunting. In this area too, identifying your target property has become more complicated as factors including the ability to work from home and a greater desire to balance work with family life have led people to look further afield for places to live. The traditional model of couples trading up within a city, or just beyond it to suburbs with excellent transport links, is increasingly being challenged by a new model that is casting the net further and has different requirements.

Buyers are therefore looking beyond familiar geographies and local markets. In other words, just like their corporate counterparts, they are heading out of their comfort and travel zones to make a strategic acquisition using new criteria.

Here, once again, the ability to enter search criteria into technology platforms and explore those options more deeply is invaluable. Yet, once that process is complete, the human desire to physically see and experience the property and its surroundings will still prevail and will ultimately drive most buying decisions.

In fact, we could justifiably conclude that, without the use of those platforms, the ability of people to make that move, or more broadly that leap of imagination, would not be possible for all but the most committed and time rich. The technology is therefore, far from replacing the human element, enabling and empowering it.

To extend the analogy one final time, it is clear that while setting the basic search criteria – price, number of bedrooms, garden, proximity to certain amenities, etc – is helpful, it may present problems. For example, it may throw up too many options in too many hard-to-compare locations or, conversely, it could too quickly repeat back the buyer's own, often limited, knowledge and assumptions, and in doing so encourage potential buyers to stick to what they know rather than think more laterally about their next move.

In this case, it's perfectly reasonable to expect a 'smart' search engine to not only take on more of the hard work, but also seek to better understand and even challenge the buyer's needs and assumptions. New and emerging technologies will increasingly be able to predict your dream property and present the results, backed up by data on your new neighbourhood, and may even include market analysis that forecasts future property price growth.

This range of technologies almost perfectly reflects those applied during the process of identifying deal targets, supporting our case that although automating the time-intensive early stages of the process may remove some human elements from the picture, this only serves to provide humans with better information to forge the relationships and decisions that only they can make.

From theory to practice: the views of a leading innovator

That's the theory, but what about the practice? In this context, we turn to Tony Qui, who is an innovation and technology leader for one of the world's largest professional service firms, focusing in particular on strategy and transactions. Not only has he played a leading role in many deals, he has also overseen the development of one of the platforms listed earlier in this chapter. For those interested in knowing more, it is described as: 'A powerful, cloud-based platform that brings ecosystems and its components to life. It can, for example, show the flow of capital and highlight past M&A activity within the sector. By doing so it visualizes the relationships between companies and shows opportunities across the sector and its value chain.'

The growing role of technology

Tony sees technology continuing to play a key and increasingly sophisticated role across the whole transaction life cycle, from strategy and target identification to deal execution and achieving post-deal synergies.

In terms of target identification specifically, he believes that banks and other major funders will continue to invest in AI to increase opportunities and mitigate risks around identifying the right target.

Tony cites the example of a PE house that runs its own data and technology-led target identification process. This process typically looks at 2,000 potential targets every year, before settling on a shortlist of 200. The PE fund came to Tony with a nagging concern that the 201st or 202nd on the list could have been the big winner that 'got away', and asked Tony to put his own lens over both the PE fund's selections and the selection process itself in order to provide both assurance and challenge.

Applying that lens meant using multiple sets of data, from news and social media to data procured from third parties and proprietary data sets. This approach was designed not only to check the accuracy of the PE fund's own shortlisting process but also to provide better insights into the criteria that the PE was applying. It's an interesting case in terms of how the two tech systems assess potential deals and how they could complement each other.

Identifying targets before they pop up

Tony also cites growing industry interest in building what he refers to as a 'deal predictive engine', which uses machine learning to train a model to predict which companies are most likely to come up for acquisition or sale. Here, the incorporation of neural networks, whose names and structures are inspired by the human brain, into the algorithms offers new possibilities and could, one day soon, provide a reliable predictive element to deal sourcing.

In terms of the ever-increasing range of data sets available, from plotting the impact of consumer trends on target companies to sifting through chat room exchanges, where does Tony think we should be looking? 'I think news is interesting. People used to look to the appointment of a CEO as a signal for sale or acquisition,' he says, but believes it's now possible and advantageous to look way below that to everything from regulatory fines to fraud and cyber breaches. 'If you are going after an asset that has a global footprint then those could impact share price and that could impact valuations,' he explains. Tony adds that the power of technology to scrape, collate and analyse words from any source – from day trader comments on social news platform Reddit to activist investor reports – is adding an extra dimension to fast and cost-effective target identification.

Eliminating bias and the use of AI

Tony's insight into being asked to use his platform to 'check the homework' of another similar platform raises a number of interesting questions. It suggests that technology platforms, rather than being agnostic and even-handed, could have inherent bias. This may be intentional because, for example, some sourcing platforms are built to favour certain target types and discount others, or it may be unintentional and accidental, just a side effect of the way the algorithm was built and trained or the data it is fed.

That's interesting because, as we discussed in Chapter 1, one of our features as humans is that we are full of biases. For example, with direct relevance to target identification, we tend to favour areas we know and understand over those we don't (so-called information bias). That's one advantage of using technology to source targets: not only is it quicker, it can also eliminate those human blind spots. Yet it seems that technology can also have similar faults.

On balance, it's likely that a deal-sourcing platform will have far less bias than a human, but it's still worth noting that it will almost certainly still have some bias. Or, if the sourcing platform is based on the same data and algorithms as its rivals, it may repeat another human failing – herd mentality.

The desire to avoid herd mentality was one of the key drivers for the proposed launch of a new venture capital fund, which proposed using AI-powered software to identify promising start-ups without relying on 'human judgement'. The selling point being that, by taking another step away from human involvement and thought processes, it could create more value. According to an article on forbes.com, published in May 2022, the founder and CEO of Revolut, Nik Storonsky, believed that 'In the bad times no one wants to invest, in the good times they all want to… there is some element of crowd mentality' (Martin, 2022). To avoid this human failing, Storonsky hired a team of data scientists and engineers to mine LinkedIn, corporate filings and other databases to identify fast-growing start-ups. 'I personally believe in having a model without having human judgment,' he said in the article. This represents a novel AI-powered approach to finding targets and an interesting angle in our debate about humans being empowered by technology. In this case, technology is being empowered to eliminate human involvement.

Black Swan, White Swan – how social data is the new gold

Steve King is CEO and co-founder of Black Swan Data, which according to its website is 'transforming unstructured data into scientific predictions'. Or, as Steve more modestly describes it to us, 'AI is giving us a way of transforming useless data into quite useful data'. Before we look at how this technology helps with target identification, it's worth understanding more about why and how the methodology developed.

In 2015, Steve's sister Julie was wheelchair-bound and in danger of losing her life. Yet, despite countless tests over several years, doctors could not find the cause. Instead of accepting this state of affairs, Steve applied his data skills. By harnessing millions of internet conversations, along with the contents of Julie's detailed diary, describing everything from what she ate to how she felt, Steve and his team started to match her symptoms with others, making connections and patterns that could not otherwise be spotted. This led to a life-changing breakthrough which meant Julie was finally diagnosed with a rare but treatable form of Parkinson's and is now able to lead a normal life with her family.

It's precisely that ability to mine the online conversations that record our needs, wants, frustrations and desires that is now yielding results for clients in the business world (although the charitable aspect of Steve's company's work lives on in sister organization, White Swan Data).

Essentially, Black Swan unlocks the power of social data to understand and predict consumer trends, using some very smart AI, NLP and deep learning models. But it doesn't stop there because it also forecasts, with a high degree of accuracy, how fast and how big those trends will go, whether it be for new types of alcoholic drinks, pet care, or snacks. Going back to our example of the nutritional supplement market, adding that predictive element to our ecosystem could be highly valuable. If, for example, you have reliable insight that the market for high-protein multi-vitamin cereal bars is going to grow rapidly, acquiring a company that makes them is not only more attractive, but less risky. And, if only you have access to this intelligence, you have a powerful advantage.

But what is the potential for this sort of insight to be applied more directly to target identification? We asked Steve, who explains that 'Looking at it from a target perspective, companies are already using our data to predict which brands are going to be interesting and they need to buy'. But he adds there is further traction in using social data, alongside stock market and other financial information, to better understand and predict the growth of companies. Steve explains that already 'Black Swan's fastest revenue arm is M&A. After all, long-term prediction is literally what deals are about and we are developing products accordingly.'

One interesting aspect of Black Swan's approach is the way that it combines the highly personal with the most highly advanced technologies, using them to discover, collate and analyse our human desires and biases. Perhaps a reflection that buying is a human process full of hidden triggers which, if scientifically understood, can be extremely powerful tools in the dealmaking process.

A tech fund leader with vision

Paul Davison is a former Rothschild investment banker and now a partner at SoftBank Vision Fund, which has assets of over $150 billion built on early stakes in tech giants such as Uber. Where does he see humans adding most value during the target identification period? He believes that at the 'top of the funnel', by which he means the early stages of potential target selection, the process has not been changed markedly by technology and is unlikely to do so in the future. 'We'll go sector by sub-sector by sub-sector in quite a granular way using information sources which aren't advanced technology but enable us to map out targets,' Paul explains. At this stage he outlines that, in terms of potential investment ideas, SoftBank gets 'a lot of inbound from earlier stage funds, other company founders, other intermediaries like banks and accounting firms, as well as our own proactive mapping'. This, of course, is an advantage of being one of the largest investment funds in the world with a recognized brand, because other investors bring deals to you and even companies who are seeking funding will approach the fund proactively.

As the potential targets proceed further down the funnel, Paul says that SoftBank has started to use more of what he calls noise or signal indicators: 'When we look at a company and it's difficult to tell from the outside how it is doing, we use signal indicators.' Although this will differ by sub-sector, he said that 'one example might be a company's hiring velocity on LinkedIn'. The common and vital element here is what he went on to describe as 'some signalling from the outside about how they're doing'. He contrasts this with news, financial reporting or surveys, which can tend to be either backwards looking or more a matter of opinion rather than being 'straight from the horse's mouth' and fact-based.

This highlights yet another area of valuable information that, while not exactly new, is becoming increasingly invaluable and accessible. The data produced by modern businesses through their normal operations can now be directly accessed to help assess their true, rather than reported, health.

Paul explains how that works: 'For consumer-facing companies like food delivery businesses, we'll look at all of the aggregated credit card data we can get hold of, enabling us to see how many people are ordering and spending on certain services. Better still, you can now look at app downloads by date and geographies and use it to explore key areas such as retention, monthly active users and overall install base.'

People are also crucial amidst these new sources of information. 'There are networks where you can speak to ex or current employees of target companies or their competitors to get first-hand anecdotal evidence about how a company's product is designed and what customers think of it,' Paul continues.

Technology won't replace human interaction

Interestingly, he sees these innovative and often technology-driven resources as the prelude to, not the replacement for, human interaction. He adds: 'Before we decide to meet a company we will try and use these resources to get a feel for how the company is doing with customers and what the company is focused on.'

SoftBank's sheer size and focus means that it is not generally in the market for early-stage investments that are yet to appear on the radar. Paul continues: 'Our mandate isn't to invest at the most fragile stage of an idea or a product or a wave of consumer behaviour; we are giving capital to founders to push the accelerator very hard. It's our job to really assess whether that company can be 100 times bigger in 10 or 20 years. Because these are very long arcs that we are trying to invest behind and that's the judgement we are making – we are trying to make an assessment on the durability and long-term market power of a company.'

Intellectual rigour crucial to SoftBank's investment philosophy

While this may seem the perfect area for the sort of AI-led, future-predictive modelling discussed earlier, Paul takes a different view. 'To make that longevity assessment,' he explained, 'we extract as much intellectual horsepower from the team as possible to think about it with as much clarity as we can. We try and step back from a story-based thesis into a data-based conclusion. For example, if we are doing a market sizing, we try to be very specific about what that size is and what is actually addressable and how much economics they are able to extract from the incumbent value chain.'

With prices high for the sort of fast-growing tech companies that Softback invariably targets, he believes that this sort of intellectual rigour is crucial.

That rigour has led him to be wary of what could be termed 'sheep in wolves' clothing', namely, companies that have positioned themselves as disruptors and in doing so have been able to attract venture capital but essentially are not fundamentally different to incumbents. He cites the insurance industry as one example, where early movers sought to create a new economic model yet some companies attracted venture funding even though 'when you assess the company on product, underwriting and distribution, they are fundamentally operating in the same way as the legacy insurers'.

He sums up the shift as follows: 'Five or 10 years ago companies that were funded by early-stage venture capital firms would offer genuinely transformative services, whereas now, ones that are not particularly disruptive are attracting this kind of capital to simply grow faster than incumbents without much meaningful prospect of achieving better unit economics over the long term.'

He sees making that call as one requiring expert human input. 'Alongside the investment team we've hired a lot of people with real operating expertise in certain segments and we will work hand-in-hand with them, particularly in investments where we think technology is a core differentiator. We ask: What is the technology advantage? Is it defensible today? How is it sustainable tomorrow?'

Paul has a wealth of investment experience and in providing an example for the point just made, he refers to a biotech drug discovery business that is using machine learning technology to parse the genome and by doing so understand how new therapies can be created. While SoftBank's operating team will contain experts who are very close to the technology, Paul explains that 'they won't use any technology methods specifically, just listening, questioning, referencing and expertise'.

Access and information are the key to target identification

Paul goes on to make a crucial and illuminating distinction: 'If you think about our job as investing in private markets, the two most important things are access and information.'

He sees access as being about relationships – the human connections that enable a potential capital provider to build a better understanding of the possible investment. 'So technology doesn't really help and isn't a big driver of that,' he explains.

On the other hand, information, in the many forms already discussed, is more technology-led, whether that be crunching the data on sectors and ecosystems or extracting signals from LinkedIn, credit card and app data. Yet, despite its undoubted power, Paul doesn't see that information as being conclusive, rather 'it pushes us towards certain companies or themes, or competitive dynamics where we understand who is winning market share and who is losing', he adds.

Summing up: power to the people

It's clear throughout this chapter that technology has a major and growing role in helping to identify potential targets for acquisition, joint ventures or partnerships. Yet to get the green light to proceed with such a deal, it appears that, from what we've learned so far, humans will still need to huddle around a table, virtual or otherwise. But when they do so they will increasingly be more confident – even in new markets, geographies or different forms of partnerships – because they will have better, deeper and more relevant information at hand, gleaned from the application of improved data and technologies.

> **KEY POINTS**
>
> - Our fast-moving, disruptive business environment is increasingly forcing companies out of their comfort zones and into unfamiliar territory as they look for the right target to help them adapt and grow.
> - The power of technology platforms to help companies cut through complexity and look beyond the obvious target candidates is proving crucial.
> - Even when they are focused on taking human instinct and bias out of the equation, technologies are enabling dealmakers to make better decisions.

- As technology develops, there is even greater potential for faster and more intuitive platforms, new predictive models and access to signals that are a better guide to a target's true, real-time performance.

References

Huang, Z, Moeller, S and Wu, E, (2022) Learning by Acquiring: The environmental and Social impact of M&A deals (working paper)

Martin, I (2022) Revolut's billionaire founder Nik Storonsky to launch AI-led venture capital fund, *Forbes*, 17 May, www.forbes.com/sites/iainmartin/2022/05/17/revolut-ceo-nik-storonsky-to-launch-ai-led-venture-capital-fund/?sh=522536262248 (archived at https://perma.cc/V5NT-VTAT)

Matthews, D (2021) Beyond Meat and Pepsi are teaming up to make plant-based snacks and drinks, *Vox*, 27 January, www.vox.com/future-perfect/2021/1/27/22252414/beyond-meat-pepsi (archived at https://perma.cc/XW6M-9HYR)

3

Winning hearts, minds and money

How keeping the seller sweet is the new secret to success, what acquirers really want, and how technology can be more human than people when it comes to negotiating

In any book or article on M&A, it's tempting to make an analogy between dealmaking and matchmaking. The parallels are appealing, from the search for a date (identifying your target, which we covered in Chapter 2) to finding out more about each other (the due diligence phase we dissect in Chapter 5), getting married (doing the deal) and living happily ever after (post-merger integration, which we dive into in Chapter 7). There's even a clear link between the technology platforms used to find acquisition targets and the dating apps used to find the right romantic partner.

So far, we've happily resisted that parallel in this book because it's a path well-trodden, but in this chapter we make an exception because it offers a useful perspective. Viewers of TV reality shows like *Love Island* (created in the UK but now formatted across the world) may already be familiar with the term 'grafting'. In this context it means that, for those looking for love, it's not enough simply to find the right match and let nature run its course; the suitor must clearly be seen to be putting in work – from supplying their prospective life partner with their favourite breakfast and morning coffee to listening carefully to their concerns and demonstrating integrity and values. So, what does this sort of grafting have to do with this chapter? The answer is that, in today's increasingly competitive and fast-moving deal world, it is often the seller who calls the shots. These sellers will need, and in fact demand, significant attention – or grafting – before there is any chance of them 'coupling up' with the acquirer.

Setting out terms

Just to get our terms clear before we go any further, this section looks at key aspects of the deal process that come after target identification but before signing the deal. This often takes place before or during due diligence, so the two parties don't necessarily have full information about each other. Critically, it's a time of building the relationships and trust as much as the exchange of facts and financials. While we acknowledge that, in a major takeover, convincing a broad set of stakeholders to back the deal (including shareholders, of course) may be crucial to its success, this isn't an area we examine in any detail here because there is little value to add in terms of our central theme of the interaction between deal technology and deal people. There are exceptions, perhaps, in how the investment case can be made more effectively and efficiently delivered by using data visualization tools and other data analytics tools, and how video calls and presentations are increasingly replacing the need for physical 'meet and greet roadshows' for investors across the world to explain the deal rationale, data, insights and approach.

Instead, in this chapter, we will examine and share our experience of the medium- and smaller-sized deals in which, typically, the major shareholder is also the founder. In these cases, the dynamics around winning hearts, minds and money are changing – and technology is playing a very strong part. These smaller deals are increasingly being used by much larger companies to expand their technology capabilities, and thus make up a significant percentage of deal activity, even in industries not traditionally considered to be based in technology.

The key drivers

As we've described in previous chapters, not only are the reasons for doing deals changing, but so are the deals themselves. Despite the headlines that tend to focus on multibillion-dollar mega-deals, the largest number of deals are made up of smaller companies being bought, often for their technology, skills or people capabilities rather than as part of a more traditional drive towards market consolidation.

While the strength of the M&A market invariably changes from year to year, typically driven by macroeconomic factors, the demand for the sort of smaller, technology and skill-rich companies described is generally high, making it a sellers' market.

Typically, in these transactions the company founders are still very much in control, even if they are not always the majority shareholder. They rightly regard having built their company as one of the most important events of their life, possibly only second to huge personal milestones such as meeting their life partner or becoming a parent. This often makes for an emotional deal process where the potential acquirers are meticulously studied by the entire sell-side deal team and specifically the founder.

Because of these factors, not only can the seller pick and choose their acquirer (because there will typically be more than one suitor), but in doing so they will be motivated to make a very careful choice in order to preserve the legacy of their creation. Note that this is true even in those cases where the founder(s) and/or significant shareholder(s) will leave their company at the time of the sale or shortly thereafter. This is because the founder is effectively selling their legacy and feels in enormous debt to the people in their organization that made the success possible. So, a big part of the pre-signing courting process is (for the target) to assess and (for the buyer) to clarify and convince the seller not only of the chances of survival but also the ongoing success of the target organization and its people.

What about the buyer? They face two problems. First, because others will almost certainly be pursuing the same target they will likely have to compete harder and pay more to secure it. Second, a potential buyer may not even get to the stage of discussing price unless they can tick all the right boxes and build a strong enough relationship with the founder.

The role of technology

So far, you may well have noticed that our argument has got everything to do with people and money and nothing to do with technology, so where does that come in? The answer is that, by helping both parties get their stories straight on the financials and other fundamentals, technology enables both the buyer and the seller to spend more time on the crucial, softer and indeed more human aspects of the deal.

For an explanation of why and how this is happening, let's go back to our Chapter 2 interview with Steve King, CEO of Black Swan Data. During our conversations, he told us how his own business has completed several rounds of investment to fund the ongoing development of its products and capabilities. He commented that by the time he got to his latest round, the process had changed substantially. The investors and their advisers had moved from more subjective methods, like interviewing Steve and other senior people to get answers on key topics, to a much more data-driven approach, governed by strict metrics. As Steve put it, rather than him supplying a small number of Excel files, the investors now 'put all our company data through a "black box", combine it with their own data and make a decision based on that'. While Steve's example may be simplifying the situation slightly, it does describe a broader trend. The collection and assessment of data has always been important when assessing a new investment but Steve's comments demonstrate what we have seen as well in terms of a market shift towards greater reliance on the data-driven answers. As Steve himself points out, this is being enabled by both the greater maturity of his business's financial systems and the increased sophistication of the tools employed by investors.

Standardization clears the runway to success

Applying that trend to our current subject, if the seller has easy access to the sort of data just described, then it will be relatively easy to provide their prospective buyers with the information they need. Note that this data has moved from being solely sourced from financial statements and increasingly comes from internal customer relationship management (CRM) systems, in-depth customer analysis but also internal and external unstructured data such as social media listening. This not only gives those buyers greater certainty and therefore confidence to bid – and likely at a higher price – it will also increase competition as all interested buyers can have access to the same information. The icing on the cake is that all of this is being achieved with less effort and more speed than previously.

Key to the readability and shareability of such information is standardization, as it enables accurate comparison and benchmarking. As financial professionals, including investment bankers, accountants, management consultants and lawyers, have evolved their skills, they have managed to provide more accurate insights into the financial and operational value of companies that were previously harder to assess because they operated in new and unfamiliar markets or involved emerging and largely unproven technologies. In addition, these professional advisers will look at softer issues such as the strength of management and the corporate culture, including the ability to retain or merge these with the buyer. But to enable useful comparison, standardization of those metrics has to occur. Fortunately, this has happened, as we'll see by taking a closer look at one particular sector.

An additional benefit of standardized metrics is that they make it much easier for even a small company with a modest finance department to produce all the key data its buyers will want to see. This may also be one of the contributing reasons to the change that we described in the introduction to this book, showing that the amount of information in the typical electronic data room was increasing dramatically even before the Covid-19 pandemic and has continued to rise. That means the seller can go to market with a full set of comprehensive information, putting them in a better position to attract buyers because they have taken away the first hurdle or, to mix metaphors, closed the information gap. Then, to return to our modern-day dating analogy, the real 'grafting' can begin.

CALLING THE SAAS: HOW STANDARDIZATION AND TECHNOLOGY ARE SUPPORTING VALUATION

Take the example of software-as-a-service (SaaS) providers. Standardized metrics such as customer numbers and acquisition costs, as well as contract values and churn rates, along with the more widely applicable key performance indicators (KPIs) like growth rates and market size, have become established within that industry, enabling comparison and providing greater assurance for investors. That opens the door for technology applications that can help the buyer and seller because, once standard metrics are in place, and clearly defined and agreed among the main stakeholders, tools can scour company financials relatively easily to find the information needed, thereby producing accurate and easily benchmarkable data.

That, in turn, makes it easier for potential buyers to get comfortable with the value of their target more quickly and perhaps to even see areas where they could add value. For example, if a company's cost to acquire a customer (CAC) is significantly below the customer's lifetime value (LTV), it suggests that the acquirer might be able to accelerate growth by investing more heavily in sales and marketing.

The KPI scorecard used by one of our authors to help SaaS acquirers identify targets and determine value is shown in full in Figure 3.1. In summary, it uses a blend of the following five KPI categories:

- annual recurring revenues (ARR) at scale in a large and growing market;
- strong 'Rule of 40' metrics (this refers to the established formula that growth rate plus cash profit margin should exceed 40 per cent);
- a pureplay SaaS business model with strong recurring revenues;
- robust client retention and net retention revenue;
- attractive sales efficiency metrics that highlight scalability.

It's important to note here that even within the SaaS sector it's not a case of one-size-fits-all. SaaS KPIs vary by end-market (such as Consumer or Enterprise) and sector (like Government, Education or Cyber). Trying to benchmark a company's performance without being aware of this sort of nuance could result in acquirers making unwise assumptions and poor decisions.

FIGURE 3.1 SaaS KPI metrics

		LOW	STRONG	LEADING	
(1) Scale of opportunity	ARR scale	< £8m	£8m – £20m	> £20m	SaaS valuation is dictated by a blend of the five KPI categories
	TAM	£500m	£500m – £2bn	> £2bn	
(2) 'Rule of 40'	ARR growth ('G')	< 20%	20% – 40%	> 40%	1) ARR scale in a large and growing market
	EBITDA margin ('M')	< –10%	–10% – 10%	> 10%	2) Strong 'Rule of 40' metrics, with an emphasis on ARR growth
	Rule of 40 ('G + M')	< 20%	20% – 40%	> 40%	3) Pureplay SaaS business model with strong recurring revenues
	Burn multiple	> 2x	2x – 1x	< 1x	
(3) Business model attractiveness	Recurring revenue %	< 70%	70% – 90%	> 90%	4) Robust client retention and NRR
	Gross margin %	< 70%	70% – 80%	> 80%	5) Attractive sales efficiency metrics that highlight scalability
	Annual contract value ('ACV')	< £30k	£30k – £80k	> £80k	
(4) Client retention	Churn % (by value)	> 13%	13% – 10%	< 10%	
	Net retention rate ('NRR')	< 100%	100% – 115%	> 115%	
(5) Sales efficiency	Customer acquisition cost ('CAC') Ratio	> 1.50	1.50 – 0.70	< 0.70	
	Lifetime value ('LTV') / CAC	< 3x	3x – 5x	> 5x	

ILLUSTRATIVE MULTIPLES OF ARR

2x – 4x	4x – 6x	6x +

SOURCE (EY internal material, 2022)

No matter how accurate and comprehensive, it's worth remembering that financial metrics will never tell the full story. That's because there are a host of qualitative rather than quantitative factors that have a big impact on business performance (and therefore valuation) but will never be fully captured by KPIs. Yet, rather than detract from the argument of this chapter, we believe this strengthens it.

To illustrate this point, we return to our dating analogy. The suitor selects their partner based on metrics designed to capture key aspects of physical appearance and personality – from height and eye colour to job and hobbies. But even the most scientific of suitors would acknowledge that matching on this basis is merely the starting point and is no guarantee of success. A relationship needs to develop. To switch back to the business world, finding a suitable target is one thing, but then discovering that it has a strong strategic fit with your own company and is led by a talented team that shares your values is equally, if not more, important.

The enduring role of the adviser

So, with metrics standardized and more easily sharable and comparable, one might think that the first human to disappear from the scene would be the adviser – at least endangered if not extinct. But counter-intuitively, and very much in line with our deal paradox, the job of the adviser actually becomes more important.

First and perhaps most important, it is the adviser that has a vast amount of experience and is supported by a team with hundreds of deals on the clock, plus access to the latest deal technology. This compares with the seller, whose team often, especially if it's a start-up, will be participating in an M&A deal for the first time.

That combination of experience and capability means the adviser brings a lot to the party:

- helping with the positioning and practicalities, like collecting, cleansing and presenting the company data as investors and acquirers expect to see it;

- using their networks to identify potential buyers and knowing what those buyers value and how they behave in processes;
- experience in running the auction process, particularly with an eye to tactics to drive the most successful deal outcome for the selling shareholders and management.

Additionally, particularly if there are multiple bidders, the adviser plays a crucial, broader role by acting as a bridge between the seller and buyer. Remember, those buyers need to impress our seller, not just with the size of their cheque book (though that helps) but, for example, with their intentions for the business, its employees and customers. This knowledge and insight are important both during an auction process to ensure you proceed with bidders that have the ability and conviction to complete the transaction, avoiding price chips or last-minute changes to the terms, and after the deal to ensure that the target employees are treated fairly. The right adviser should be able to provide insights here and navigate the process and conversations with a focus on where the value lies for both parties. Clever deal management systems such as DealCloud can now gather important intelligence on buyer behaviour at each stage of the deal process and utilize it to improve results in future processes.

So that puts the adviser right in the middle of both the technology and people aspects of the deal process. By making sure the buyers have the data they need, and in a form that the buyers can not only access but investigate, for example through data visualization tools, the adviser encourages more buyers to engage. The adviser can then respond to buyer queries and also ask their own questions of the buyer to make sure that the potential acquirer not only has the financial resources necessary but also aligns with the seller's objectives.

An industry insider explains the need for advisers

Andrew Binstead is head of Corporate Development at IFS, a major European software company working with some of the world's largest businesses. His team typically buy four or more companies a year, so it's particularly interesting that, when buying smaller and often founder-led start-up companies, he told us that he prefers the seller be represented by an experienced adviser.

Andrew explains: 'There are three key benefits. First, a good adviser will increase the pace and certainty of the process – frequently this will be the first time that the seller will have sold a company. That adviser will make sure that the seller is aware of all the issues that have to be addressed in the deal, which means that it is less likely that a showstopper will arise toward the end of the negotiation and approval process (or that a "standard" deal mechanic becomes an emotive obstacle, because the seller doesn't understand what is going on).

'Second, having a channel with an adviser allows the opportunity to explore creative ways round impasses – every time I open my mouth with a seller I am perceived to be negotiating; sometimes it's important to have off-the-record discussions to understand what is behind an issue and "fly a kite" on possible options without committing. Third, advisers can leverage experience from other deals to find value-creating solutions – their main aim is to maximize value for their client, but an experienced adviser can play a key role in creating a win-win deal for both sides.'

Boosting the bids: adding value in auctions

In many cases there will be a bilateral negotiation between two parties, but in this instance we want to address the situation when, having got multiple buyers interested, our adviser would then organize the auction process to tease out from the market the best buyer at the best price. This auction process essentially aims to bring several potential bidders through the full length of the deal process up to the point where the final buyer is selected and the terms of the deal are finalized. In highly competitive auctions, it is not unusual to keep optionality (regarding who will win the auction to buy the target company) all the way to the point when the transaction documents are signed, that is, exclusivity will never be given to any bidder, even when a preferred party has been identified.

Technology is playing an important role here because, to ensure a competitive auction, you want to present a highly desirable target company and then encourage several highly motivated bidders to 'run hard'. But that outcome requires a lot of input and management's time is never scarcer and at more of a premium than during a company sale process. Fortunately, technology is now able to leverage management's prepared materials to a wider audience (such as through pre-recorded management presentations or real-time product demonstrations, at least in the earlier stage of an auction process). Running most of the interactions between the deal teams using video conferencing tools ensures a higher participation of decision makers and in many cases more efficient due diligence. But as we will see in the real deal examples in this book, the need for in-person meetings hasn't disappeared but has instead been elevated to premium status.

Taking care of baby: selling a highly personal business

That's enough of the theory, let's look at the practicalities of a deal.

In 2021, the founder-owners of a group comprising three different but related brands were looking to exit their businesses: CREATE Fertility (one of the UK's leading providers of IVF services with clinics across Britain), sister company abc IVF (supplier of innovative lower-cost fertility treatments), and Denmark-based IVF clinic Vitanova. As a successful and growing enterprise with strong market positions as providers of more natural, low-intervention fertility treatment, the businesses were always likely to attract a lot of interest. A key point to mention is their commitment to medical excellence. CREATE Fertility founder, Professor Geeta Nargund, is a pioneer in the field who also holds a senior position at a leading London hospital and her opinions on fertility matters are regularly sought by the specialist and mainstream press (WeAreTechWomen, 2018*)*.

With Natural Life Sciences a particularly hot sector at the time that the deal was being negotiated and with CREATE Fertility holding a strong and growing position in that particular market, both of the principal deal advisers knew they were in a strong position to find their clients the right buyer at the right price.

Remote conditions support a more personal approach

One potential hiccup was that the sale process was taking place during the Covid-19 pandemic lockdowns, limiting the ability for both parties to meet face to face. Potentially, this was a major hurdle for both sides, particularly as the sellers were keen to find the right fit for the business to which they had dedicated so much of their lives and had seen help so many men and women achieve their dreams of becoming parents. In short, they wanted to hand on the mantle to someone who knew and understood their business, including the important emotional aspects related to their customers. This made them choose a trade sale, rather than IPO or private equity buyout, as they felt such a buyer would have more insight into what made CREATE special and a more similar, science-based corporate culture.

To cut to the chase, one buyer very quickly established themselves as a serious contender, not only because of the strategic fit but also what one of the deal advisers describes as a 'meeting of minds'.

That buyer was Spain-based IVIRMA Global, the world's largest reproductive health services provider, which was looking to transform its UK market presence (Willems, 2021). Just as importantly, IVIRMA was also founded and run by medical experts with a long history of innovative, research-led practice within the infertility sector. 'It was clear that there was a lot of respect, common ground and admiration between the buyer and seller from the beginning,' explains the deal adviser. That didn't mean there weren't plenty of hurdles to overcome, including a great deal of due diligence, given the complexities inherent in the science and the IP aspects of the deal. Rather than hinder due diligence, the lack of physical meet-ups often helped. 'It was relatively easy to get everyone together on a call to discuss any issue that came up, which would have been harder and taken much longer if a physical meeting was held instead,' adds the adviser. The presence of even the most senior stakeholders in meetings made it much easier to progress the deal in virtual calls, providing reassurance, increasing speed and showing the commitment of the buyers.

In some cases, physical connection is still the clincher

Interestingly, some aspects of the deal could not be done virtually. The buy-side insisted on visiting some of the CREATE clinics in person, even though it meant flying over to the UK and quarantining in a hotel room as the Covid-19 guidelines stipulated at the time. Perhaps, with the deal world sometimes compared to a high-stakes poker game, this move could be classified being as a new type of 'tell' (an action that unintentionally gives away the strength of a player's hand). After all, few buyers would go to the trouble of spending several days alone in a budget hotel room if they weren't fully intending to do the deal.

Not only was the bidder, IVIRMA, a perfect fit in terms of trust and intentions, it was also a perfect fit commercially. That in turn made them willing to pay a higher price than other bidders because that perfect fit meant that the value that they could create post-deal was greater, including synergies. The acquisition would mean that all CREATE Fertility's services could potentially be sold across IVIRMA's global platform. This nicely dovetails not only with IVIRMA's ambition to increase customers and revenues but also the founders' original motivations. 'Our aim has always been to help as many patients as possible access natural, mild and affordable IVF treatments and IVIRMA's global platform will help us achieve exactly that,' stressed Professor Nargund when commenting on the deal in UK news publication *CITY A.M.* (Willems, 2021).

One final interesting aspect to mention regarding the deal is that one of the advisers who worked on the deal was so impressed by the selling management – and the feeling was mutual – that he has now joined their newly set up investment entity as a fund manager. In other words, the deal not only won the hearts and minds of the participants but also the adviser helping to manage it!

It also illustrates how technology-enabled virtual communications can still provide valuable insights into human behaviours. It's not uncommon to assign one deal team member to do nothing else other than watch and interpret the body language of the key players during Zoom or Teams calls to gain intelligence. It is a widely held view that such behaviours are often far more revealing of a buyer's true intent than what they actually say on those video calls or write in emails. While acknowledging the advantages of video calls, such as saving time and enabling 'air time' to be spread more evenly across the participants, it is worth noting that their success in the deal process may in part be due to the fact that key players have already built up trust through pre-pandemic relationships. The danger then is that such meetings could, to some extent, exclude new entrants without a previous connection and therefore slow down the process.

Finally, the 'happy ending' we saw as the adviser joined the acquirer reminds us that, as we wrote in the introductory chapter, deals have a lot in common with stories. This includes having clear stages or 'acts' and many unpredictable twists and turns on the way to a final resolution. But most relevant to this chapter is that stories must also engage. A fictional narrative can have all the right elements in the right place yet somehow fail to grab the audience and therefore fail to engage. The parallel with this stage of the deal process is clear, as there often needs to be a connection or engagement that goes beyond the facts and financials. The growing importance of collaboration, and how it is reshaping deal culture, is explored in our concluding chapter, *The future of the deal*.

The role of negotiation and who does it best

What we've explored so far is how winning hearts, minds and money is about much more than setting up easily interrogated information, opening smart data rooms and starting bidding wars. It's also about building trust and getting comfortable about each other's intentions.

That description could also apply to the negotiation process, which of course is itself key to winning hearts, minds and money. In the next chapter we will talk about deal price but, although that tends to be the sole focus of the newspaper headline writers, any dealmaker knows it is generally only one part of a complex negotiating process. Looked at in the round, nearly every step of the way between identifying targets and signing the deal involves negotiation of sorts.

We're also interested in negotiation because it's a touchstone of human instinct and behaviour. What could be more human-centric than sitting at a table opposite your counterparty and playing your hand carefully but decisively to win? Not only is it seen as a key and perhaps irreplaceable human function, but it inevitably draws us towards the traditional stereotype of a tight-lipped, square-jawed alpha male (as they will inevitably be masculine in this paradigm), playing his cards close to his chest, while looking you in the eye and never blinking. But is any of it true? And even if so, is it useful?

The machine that negotiates

To find out more, our last interview for this chapter is with a man who lived and breathed these types of negotiations before building his own technology to do it better. Martin Rand is the CEO of Pactum, an AI system that unlocks value by automating negotiations. He began his career as a product manager at Skype before setting up his first company, VitalFields. This was acquired by global agri-business Monsanto, who then recruited him to their previously acquired Climate Corporation division, where he conducted many complex negotiations all over the world. As well as holding a master's degree in IT Management, he has studied advanced negotiations at Harvard University.

Martin explains that the idea for Pactum was born, 'like many good ideas, out of pain'. The catalyst was a particularly frustrating negotiation in which, well into the negotiation process, the other side made a number of significant and non-negotiable demands which they declared must all be met in their entirety before talks could progress. Martin's side quickly saw it would not be possible to meet these demands and that was the end of that deal. 'I thought, wow, how unprofessional was that on both sides? All this time spent when a deal was never going to be reached? And how much money was left on the table,' he explains, adding that the reasons for such an impasse were depressingly familiar: 'cultural differences, complexity, cognitive biases and, crucially, a lack of planning and preparation – all of the usual stuff, which hinders good negotiations outcomes.'

Even when negotiations fared better, he still realized that money was being left on the table, often simply because there was just too much detail for humans to grasp.

Pactum was then launched in 2019 because Martin believes 'technology can go through more data than humans, it can fully prepare for even the smallest negotiation, it can deal with huge complexities – and do it all faster.' He cites a simple example to support his argument: the annual contract. Why is a contract only set or revised annually when everything that underpins it – from commodity prices to supply chains – changes daily? The answer, Martin believes, is that 'it's a way for humans to be able to do something only once per year then forget it for 12 months'. But, as he points out, machines don't have these kinds of limitations and can renegotiate the contract as often as desirable, for example with every fluctuation of commodity spot prices, and without significant costs.

So Martin is using his AI-powered tool to break new ground by, for example, helping logistics companies set a contract for a single container while it's still at sea. That means being able to respond to changing costs and demands, rather than being locked into a contract set months ago and probably, in order to reduce complexity, on the same terms as all the other containers on board the ship.

What does this tell us about M&A – and people?

So, what does this have to do with M&A? After all, Pactum mainly deals with high-volume customer–supplier contracts. Well, as it turns out, there is a lot we can learn.

First, there is the general point that M&A deal negotiations are often very complex, with lots of moving parts. That makes them very hard for humans to manage effectively and the reason why, as a rule, we tend to – consciously or not – focus on one or a few key areas, ignoring the rest.

To make matters worse, we tend to, according to Martin, choose those most likely to cause conflict. 'People have a hard time with complexity, so they pick two or three items that are most important to them and then try to maximize those. But in fact, the way to maximize an outcome of a deal is to find the optimal solution for the full combination of items.'

Those limits to humans' processing power also cause other problems within deal negotiations. 'People try to cut corners. They don't spend enough time in the discovery phase in the beginning of getting to know each other and finding out what is important for the other side,' explains Martin.

That's interesting because it sounds a lot like the empathy and understanding that we all tend to believe is something that only people can provide. Instead, Martin seems to be suggesting that, in this case at least, machines are better at 'being human' than we are.

He also raises the question of experience. Again, it's something which we like to believe humans are good at building up and applying. Martin sees it differently: 'For the seller and in some cases the buyer, this may be the first deal they've done, so they are embarking on a hugely important event with absolutely no practical experience. The advantage of Pactum technology is that it is constantly negotiating and can learn from every deal. Machines have the inbuilt ability to learn – and every past or current negotiation makes every future negotiation better.'

While one way to overcome this might be by hiring an experienced adviser with a vast back history of deals to draw on, Martin has his doubts. He cites what he calls 'the agency problem', where the values of the agent (in this case the adviser) are not aligned to the deal participants. He means that the agent may be overinvested in completing the deal, because essentially that is their role and how they make their living. 'The entrepreneur might be ready to let the deal go if it's not right because there will be another one, but the agent will definitely want to get the deal done,' he explains. The counter-argument, of course, is that any good adviser will always act dispassionately in the interests of their client, but we all know instances where selfish human nature has taken over, even despite the best of intentions.

Human advantages over machines

Martin does believe that human intelligence has some distinct advantages when it comes to negotiations. As he points out in a recent *Forbes* article: 'These include strategic negotiations, which benefit from human sensitivity. For example, people can anticipate cultural differences, get a gut feeling about the other party and back-channel information to save a deal that is at risk of going south. Machines cannot negotiate things that are not officially on the table – only people can think outside the box' (Rand, 2021a). But before we get too carried away with our human abilities and their central place in M&A, it's important to remember that, as we found in Chapter 1, although 'thinking out of the box' and bold strategic moves may be positive game changers during the deal process, they can also prove to be hugely destructive. In such circumstances, technology's ability to provide checks and balances or even a sandbox for testing ideas, mean it still has a role to play.

The hybrid approach: human and machine

So, with Martin's long experience of both human and machine negotiation, what does he think is the best way to approach them?

'The first thing most people think about when they start negotiating is how to increase their side's share of the pie,' he says, adding that this is the wrong way to go. Instead, it's best to focus on what he calls 'expanding the pie', by which he means increasing the value of the whole deal. 'And you do that by thinking about the other side, thinking how to maximize the value for the other side,' Martin explains.

He then breaks it down further: 'The first step could be everything on the table. So let's talk about our interests and talk about everything we could negotiate.' Martin believes humans are best at getting this going but then, with everything on the table, the number of possibilities and combinations means that machines are better at identifying optimum outcomes.

Martin also has some interesting observations about the qualities needed by negotiators, which resonate with our exploration of the subject so far. Rather than the combative, gunslinger negotiator style often favoured in popular fiction, movies and television shows, Martin believes that successful negotiators actually hold pretty much opposite characteristics. That is, successful dealmakers are collaborative, cooperative and, through being more empathetic, better able to understand what the counterparty wants and why.

The gender factor: do women do better deals?

His interest in these qualities led Martin to carefully examine the value of female and male attributes in negotiations. He cites 2017 research from Laura Kray of the University of California, Berkeley, and Jessica Kennedy of Vanderbilt University, which found that 'women possess unique advantages as negotiators, including greater cooperativeness and stronger ethics. But often those strengths are overlooked or severely undervalued, and often mostly so by women themselves' (Rand, 2021b).

Gender Diversity and Dealmaking 2022, published by the M&A Research Centre at Bayes Business School, City, University of London, SS&C Intralinks and Mergermarket, shows how these different attributes may influence M&A deals (Anderman, 2022). It found that the types of acquisitions undertaken by acquirers with female CEOs and 30 per cent or more female representation on boards are significantly different from those conducted by male CEOs or less diverse boards. They are more likely to seek advice, more risk-averse and tend to seek out targets with stronger performance metrics. Perhaps as a result of this approach, more diverse boards and female CEOs also produce better results post-deal than their male counterparts across several key indicators such as share price performance, return on equity (ROE), EBIT/sales (earnings before interest and taxes/sales) and EBITDA/sales (earnings before interest, taxes and depreciation/sales). Yet, paradoxically, deals conducted by female CEOs are still viewed less favourably by the financial markets than those conducted by their male counterparts.

The study finds that market-adjusted acquirer share price returns were 1.5 percentage points lower for deals where the acquirer had a female CEO compared to those where the acquirer was led by a male CEO, when looking at a 40-day window around the announcement date.

Towards a more diverse dealmaker

That's interesting because it chimes with our findings that, as technology takes a lot of the 'hard slog' out of the deal process, makes work and home life more compatible and closes the information gap, the culture of dealmaking is shifting towards a more open and collaborative approach. On balance, we see it as less about gender (not all women would necessarily conform to that collaborative ideal, just as not all men would fit the lone, tight-lipped alpha-male stereotype) and more about that change in culture. While, on a personal level, we welcome that shift, it's important to note that's not purely because it makes the deal world fairer and more inclusive; we also welcome it because of its potential to drive better deals with better outcomes. And similarly, although winning hearts and minds requires the virtues of tact, understanding and trust, it is ultimately still all about the pursuit of the prize and cash. As any hard-grafting *Love Island* contestant understands only too well.

KEY POINTS

- In hot sectors where it's a seller's market, winning the trust of your target can be vital to clinching the deal.
- Human connection is clearly key to winning hearts and minds, but technology is a key enabler, making the selection and initial due diligence process easier and more objective (thus less emotional), thereby freeing up key players to build trust.
- As both can destroy value if left unchecked, avoid making assumptions about what humans can do and machines can't.
- As dealmaking culture shifts to a more collaborative approach, it brings with it the potential to drive better deals with better outcomes.
- Technology can sometimes be more 'human' than people.

References

Anderman, D (2022) Gender Diversity and Dealmaking 2022: Research Results. *SS&C*, 25 May, www.ssctech.com/blog/gender-diversity-and-dealmaking-2022-research-results-1 (archived at https://perma.cc/AY2H-DF68)

Rand, M (2021a) Companies are adopting AI for supplier negotiations, but which ones should the machines handle? *Forbes*, 13 March, www.forbes.com/sites/martinrand/2021/03/26/women-have-unique-advantages-as-negotiators-how-can-they-best-leverage-them/?sh=5f8a0fab2dac (archived at https://perma.cc/G5KK-3H87)

Rand, M (2021b) Women have unique advantages as negotiators, *Forbes*, 26 March, www.forbes.com/sites/martinrand/2021/03/26/women-have-unique-advantages-as-negotiators-how-can-they-best-leverage-them/?sh=5f8a0fab2dac (archived at https://perma.cc/PFH5-BLYY)

WeAreTechWomen (2018) Inspirational woman: Professor Geeta Nargund-Founder and medical director of CREATE fertility, *WeAreTechWomen*, 7 July, https://wearetechwomen.com/inspirational-woman-professor-dr-geeta-nargund-founder-medical-director-create-fertility/ (archived at https://perma.cc/ZG3C-UQDK)

Willems, M (2021) Sale of CREATE Fertility marks biggest deal in UK's IVF sector ever, *City A.M.*, 29 July, www.cityam.com/sale-of-create-fertility-marks-biggest-deal-in-uks-ivf-sector-ever/ (archived at https://perma.cc/GY8E-HHZS)

4

Priced to perfection

How technology is playing a growing role in both the art and science of setting a deal price

What better way to begin our exploration of deal pricing as human art or data-driven science than through a brief foray into the contemporary art world?

In 2017, an untitled work by artist Jean-Michel Basquiat sold for $110.5 million, far exceeding auctioneer Sotheby's estimate. That made it not only the most expensive painting ever by an American artist but also, at the time of sale, the highest price paid for any artwork created after 1980 (Pogrebin and Reyburn, 2017). In fact, even in 2021, it was one of the 10 most expensive artworks of all time sold at auction (Villa, 2021).

How the artwork reached such a lofty price is only partially down to calculable factors. The previous year, another untitled Basquiat painting had sold for $57.3 million, indicating a very strong demand for his work (Villa, 2021). His untimely death at the age of 27 from a heroin overdose meant that no new works would ever be created, meaning that supply was finite. According to the Citi Global Art Market, contemporary art delivered an average 14 per cent annual return between 1995 to 2020 (McKeever, 2021), this suggested to investors and art lovers alike that there is a strong potential for future capital returns.

But none of this really explains why the eye-watering price of $110.5 million was reached on that day for that particular work of art. Human factors were certainly at play, with two powerful bidders competing in the pressured atmosphere of an auction, and there was also the likelihood that the winner had already made a strong personal connection with the painting. This was confirmed on Instagram when Japanese billionaire Yusaku Maezawa revealed himself as the buyer, explaining that 'when I first encountered this painting, I was struck with so much excitement'.

At first glance, the business world would appear to have precious little in common with the rarefied atmosphere of the art world but, then again, the two have more similarities than first meets the eye:

- No two companies are the same, just as no two paintings are the same. The uniqueness of the opportunity to buy a company, and also to stop others from doing the same, mirrors the one-off nature of the purchase of each painting.
- The competitive tension of the art auction is similar to that of the deal process, with some bidders active and others biding their time, some known to the other bidders and others not, and some bidders only appearing at the last minute.
- In both the worlds of art and M&A dealmaking, there is a tendency to let emotions drive decision making, as we saw in Chapter 1, where we introduced the various behavioural finance issues.
- Finally, as we will go on to examine in this chapter, there are a large number of complexities and vagaries around the valuation of a target company. This suggests that, as with the market for paintings, deal pricing can be considered as much an art as it is a science.

It also indicates that the all-important pricing element of deals should prove to be fertile ground for our exploration into the way technology is adding value in every aspect of the deal process, yet by doing so it supports rather than eliminates human decision makers.

The gap between value and price

First, let's clarify the distinction between price and value. We know the price of the aforementioned painting – but what about its value? Intrinsically, it is made of wood, canvas, and paint, all of which hold little or no value. There is also the 'human and emotional' value the buyer gets from owning and looking at it, which few would dispute is hard if not impossible to measure in monetary terms and importantly will differ for each buyer. There is also the empirical and undisputed market valuation based on the actual sale prices recently paid for similar, but critically, not identical pieces of artwork. But, even when left to experts at one of the world's finest auction houses who set the estimated prices for works that come up for sale, those comparable prices often bear little relation to its hammer price as indeed happened in the case of the Basquiat, which sold for almost 200 per cent more than its pre-sale estimate of $40 million (Villa, 2021).

In deals in the business world, the definition of value is, thankfully, a little clearer. Broadly speaking, there is:

- the value of the assets the target company owns;
- its market value according to its share price (if publicly listed);
- its relative value in comparison to other similar companies;
- the value that is generated by the company itself in terms of current and future profits.

Those valuation methodologies can vary widely from each other and will be significantly affected by certain assumptions (such as the choice of which companies are close comparisons or the estimates of what the future profits will be). Investment bankers are paid large sums to do these valuations. But if several are asked to provide the price that the company can expect to achieve when bought, the range of possible amounts will usually be wide. As famous US investor Warren Buffett puts it, 'Price is what you pay, value is what you get' (Booth, 2022).

What Buffett means by this is that while the price of a company's shares, a bar of gold or even a can of soda is arbitrary, pushed up and down by an almost endless list of factors, value is fundamental. Someone like Buffett buys shares at today's prices because he believes their intrinsic value (based on future earnings and other factors) is higher.

So, while value is not the same as price, it can, in the wider context of dealmaking at least, prove a valuable foundation or benchmark for it. These estimates can also affect the seller's willingness to sell, or the buyer's willingness to buy. Yet, while there is much more to explore in terms of value and valuation methods, it's already clear from the points just made that those looking for scientific certainty are likely to be disappointed and those more at home in the art market – familiar with the importance of human emotion and the uncertainty of clear information – may turn out to have useful transferable skills.

Through the looking glass: the vagaries of valuation

Most M&A advisers will kick off the valuation process by calculating the intrinsic value of the target company, which in theory at least is an objective process using financial calculations. The starting point usually involves making comparisons between the company up for sale and other similar companies recently sold, assuming you're lucky enough to have such recent comparable transactions. Yet, no two companies are exactly the same, so some form of standard measurement is required to make a useful comparison.

These typically take the form of multiples. At the most simple level, a multiple may signify how much a similar firm was sold for in relation to its annual profits, annual sales or its assets… or indeed all of these. Apply that multiple to your target firm's profits, for example, and hey presto – you've got a starting figure. But it is clear even at this stage of our exploration that this is unlikely to be entirely satisfactory. Because, of course, there are multiple ways of determining even this simple calculation. It may sound simple to start with, say, annual profits. But then the choices need to be made. Do we start with last year's profits or an average of the prior two or three years? Or if the company's net income is growing or shrinking, do we use a forecast of the current or next year's profit figures? And if forecasted, which set of numbers (from the company's management team or from independent analysts)? Should we adjust the profit figures to account for how the buyer would make changes to the company? Do we use pre- or post-tax figures? Are there one-time factors in the historical profit figures that may not recur or that may change in the future? And these are just some of the questions to ask about what seemed to be a simple, sometimes independently audited annual profit figure.

Based on this metric alone, a company with very valuable assets and relatively small profits risks going for a song while a highly profitable company with few assets and no 'moat' to protect it from competitors might be hugely overvalued. This has helped fuel the development of other metrics (see Figure 4.1), including multiples based on earnings before interest, taxes, depreciation and amortization (EBITDA), free cash flow, revenue, or even in the pre-profit and sometimes pre-revenue tech start-up world, where alternative valuation methods have used customer numbers or so-called 'eyeballs on screens', as was common when the internet boom started in the late 1990s.

FIGURE 4.1 The bewildering range of valuation methods

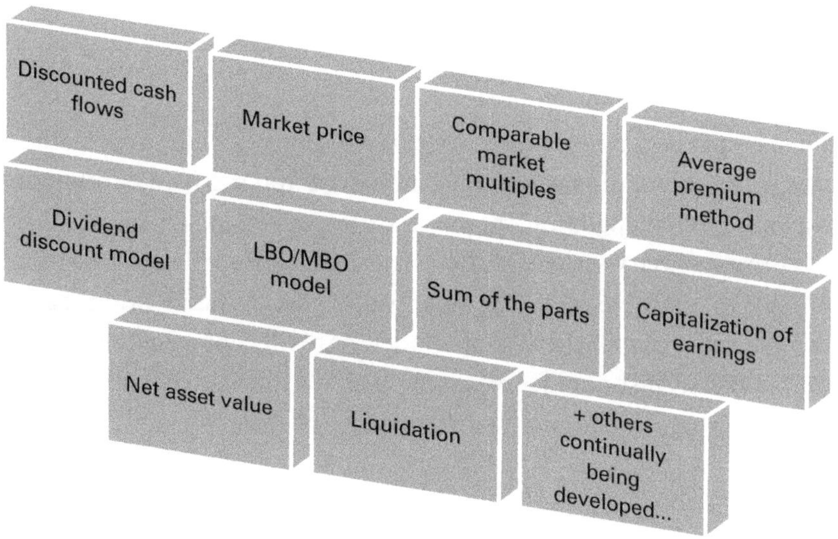

- Discounted cash flows
- Market price
- Comparable market multiples
- Average premium method
- Dividend discount model
- LBO/MBO model
- Sum of the parts
- Capitalization of earnings
- Net asset value
- Liquidation
- + others continually being developed...

It would be no exaggeration to say that there is an entire industry and several libraries' worth of literature dedicated to defining and discussing valuation methods. Yet, no matter how technically astute, innovative and business-friendly the methodology, the fact that there are so many different ones, all of which will almost certainly generate different figures, rather undermines their collective case. Further uncertainty is created by the ever-changing nature of valuation metrics. When Facebook bought WhatsApp in 2014 for $19 billion, the acquired company had $20 million in revenue (Malay Mail, 2014), representing an eye-watering multiple of 950 times revenue, exceeded perhaps only by some of the prices paid for other start-up companies that didn't even have any revenues yet.

> TECHNOLOGY-DRIVEN VALUATION DISPARITIES
>
> Since the late 1990s with the development of the then-new internet, M&A deals and even IPOs have ripped up the value rule books. For example, at the time of writing, Airbnb is worth more than Hilton, Marriott and Hyatt combined, with all of their hotel assets (Suria, 2021). These valuation disparities continue, driven by the impact of digitalization on company value and the moves in the direction of the greening of the economy, to mention just two trends. At one point in 2020, not only was the market value of Tesla much greater than General Motors, but also larger than the combined market capitalization of the next 10 largest publicly listed car companies (including Toyota, BYD of China, Volkswagen, Mercedes-Benz, BMW, General Motors and Ford) (Richter, 2021).

This supports the hypothesis that, while current valuation methodologies are certainly useful, they should be applied with caution and constantly challenged on the basis of logic, rationality and realism. On our imaginary scorecard, despite the inroads made so far by technology to improve valuation methodologies, humans are ahead in this process because there is no model that will capture all the factors that make, as just noted, Tesla (which sold around a half million cars in 2020) worth so much more than General Motors (which sold approximately 2.5 million cars that year in the US alone) (Hoium, 2021).

> LIVING IN A MATERIAL WORLD: ESG AND THE FUTURE OF VALUATION
>
> Companies need to be alert to new ways of valuation, many of which are now being driven by ESG-related factors and supported by technology and data. In an article from Bloomberg in late 2022, JPMorgan, the largest US bank, was described as teaming up with software firm Datamaran 'to develop a data analysis tool for clients to gauge not just the environmental, social and governance risks facing portfolio companies, but also the ESG risks that such assets pose to the world around them in a relatively new analytical method known as "double materiality"' (Ritchie, 2022).
>
> The article also stressed the importance of looking forwards when it comes to valuation. 'If you limit your views to things that are currently financially material, by definition you are going to miss the ones that are soon going to become financially material,' Jean Xavier Hecker, the Paris-based co-head of EMEA ESG research at JPMorgan and the architect behind their new tool, said in an interview. Although the tool was designed for asset management companies and their portfolios, it's easy to see how it could be applied in M&A deal valuation.

Don't forget deal costs

Just as the cost of buying and moving into a house isn't just the price paid to the seller (as the buyer will also typically need to pay the real estate agents, lawyers, building inspectors, surveyors, and movers) purchasing a company has additional costs as well to add on top of the price paid to the owners of the target company. Therefore, before we go on to look at the future role of technology for the art of valuation, it's worth noting that the full list of costs to the acquirer of actually doing the deal must also be taken into account in the deal price (see Figure 4.2). These costs can be considerable, from advisers' fees and funding costs (typically ranging from 3–5 per cent of the

FIGURE 4.2 The many cash costs of an acquisition

Investment banking fees	• Advisory fees • Expenses
Legal fees	• Advisory fees • Due diligence • Expenses
Accountant fees	• Due diligence • Verification of projected revenues and expenses • Post-deal integration preparation
Interest payments on debt	• Long-term financing • Bridge loans
Other fees	• Public relations • Proxy agents • Brokerage • Various specialist consultancies (strategy, pension, IT, etc)

purchase price and due at closing) to the usually hefty expense of integrating the two companies after the deal closes (perhaps as much as 15 per cent of that purchase price, albeit spread over several years). On top of those cash outgoings, there's also the opportunity cost of doing the deal rather than investing resources elsewhere and the distraction that the deal will cause to management, employees, salespeople and others. It's no surprise that the acquirer may need to raise new money or take on additional debt (sometimes as a bridging loan) to finalize the deal. On top of this, if the target company has debts, these must also be taken into account.

Using technology to power pricing

At this stage of our examination of deal pricing, what we might call the nursery slopes or the foothills of the process, technology is already hard at work but can certainly go faster and find new routes.

At present, as noted above, multiples including various profit measures such as the commonly used EBITDA are calculated from precedent deals and then applied to the financial performance of the target company to try to determine the intrinsic value of the target firm. What's relatively new is that technology is being used not only to extract that information from public and private sources but also to carry this out in real time to create a live and constantly updating EBITDA database. Existing technologies are already capable of accurately collating and predicting the costs associated with deals, based not only on standards set by other deals but increasingly by using the actual but ever-changing data for the deal itself.

As discussed, comparisons with similar companies are one of the keys to valuation, and here vast data indexing can do the legwork to help to find the closest comparable firms, which is not always evident from the PR material put out by each company itself and which often contains 'spin' on the positive factors whilst downplaying the negatives. It is also possible to use machine learning and back-testing techniques to better assess the accuracy of the target's financial and accounting reporting systems, which could identify any operational issues and risks the target is facing, as well as any potential biases due to managerial and other human factors. These considerations would then be accompanied by suitable adjustments to the deal valuation and pricing.

The analysis can also be used to influence the expectations of the seller, by providing real-time and documented data. In addition, the ability to dissect more data faster and more accurately should enable the deal process to proceed more efficiently, especially in a situation where both parties want the deal to go ahead and are willing to share information and the output of the machine learning systems. As less than 3 per cent of all deals annually are unsolicited or hostile, this means that such information sharing has the potential to be used in the vast majority of deals (Faelten et al, 2016).

One key element of pricing we haven't yet discussed is intangible assets such as brand value, customer loyalty, human capital, and supplier relationships. These are of huge importance. In fact, it is calculated by some analysts that up to 90 per cent of the value of the

S&P 500 lies in intangible assets that are notoriously hard to quantify using traditional metrics (Ali, 2020). Here, the industrial internet of things, NLP and other machine learning techniques are beginning to be used to evaluate important intangible assets and incorporate those additional factors into the deal valuation and pricing process. Examples might include technologies that use social media data to judge how well a company's ESG stance is perceived by its customers or its attractiveness as a place to work.

Are we missing something big?

We have got this far without addressing the elephant in the room and the factor that makes deal pricing so fascinating and (yet even more) complex. Remember our introduction about contemporary artwork and how a key factor in the price struck was how much it meant to the individual buyer? There is a parallel in the business world, but thankfully it's one that is easier to quantify.

Essentially, a buyer is unlikely to go to all the trouble and cost of acquiring a company unless they believe that they can create even more value from it, usually through combining it with their existing business. In other words, through these synergies, the whole will be greater than the sum of the parts. For example, an acquisition may add extra products or services which can be sold through existing distribution channels, thereby increasing revenues and broadening markets while also cutting costs because, in this example, only one sales operation is required. Or on the cost side, the acquirer can eliminate duplicated expenses in support functions (finance, HR, operations, etc), and there can even be tax and other financial synergies. These synergies will vary widely depending on the nature of the prospective acquirer and, therefore, so will the price they are willing to pay. So, not only will the 'objective' valuations vary according to the methodology, so will the value of the target company according to the individual make-up and objectives of each buyer. A buyer who has more synergies will typically be willing to pay a higher price as they will be able to offset that higher price against those larger synergy savings.

Let's look at an example of how synergies vary between buyers and how that can impact deal pricing.

> **DIALLING IN THE SYNERGIES: WHY ONE TELECOMS GIANT'S BARGAIN CAN BE ANOTHER'S NO GO**
>
> As the final year of the last millennium dawned, a battle royale was about to break out in what was then the white heat of emerging technology: mobile phones. US telecom Bell Atlantic (now known as Verizon) was in hot pursuit of US mobile phone company AirTouch Communications and had offered $73 per share, representing a deal price of $45 billion. Bell Atlantic's stock price fell 5 per cent on the announcement, suggesting that shareholders thought it was paying too much, even though that $73 only represented a 7 per cent premium to AirTouch's pre-offer deal price (Eccles et al, 1999), a discount on the usual offer premiums of between 20 and 40 per cent.
>
> Clearly, Vodafone thought differently, because a few days later the UK telcoms giant bid $55 billion for AirTouch, or $89 per share, subsequently raising it to $93 per share to finally secure the target for $62 billion. Yet, despite paying a third more than Bell Atlantic's initial offer (and within the range of the normal offer premium level), Vodafone's share price actually rose by around 15 per cent during the bidding war (Deseret News, 1999).
>
> The reason for the disparity was the greater synergies that Vodafone could realize from the deal. As Vodafone had a much larger share of the European cellular market than Bell Atlantic, this meant that the acquisition would immediately create the first complete pan-European cellular telephone company. By contrast, a combined Bell Atlantic-AirTouch operation would not have created such a pan-European company, so it had far less potential moving forwards.
>
> That explains the strategic synergy for Vodafone, but there were cost synergies too. The new combined company would be able to save on the fees paid as calls crossed networks, avoid duplication of backroom tasks, and achieve greater economies of scale when purchasing equipment. In summary, Vodafone paid more for AirTouch for the simple reason that it was worth more to Vodafone than it was to the other bidders.

As this example neatly illustrates, not only do anticipated synergies need to be factored into the acquirer's offer price, the seller must recognize that each buyer will have different potential synergies and adjust their price expectations accordingly. Technology has a key role to play here, not only drawing on rich data sources to more quickly and accurately calculate and model synergies but perhaps also to identify and model previously unseen opportunities for synergies. We'll look at some examples of how technology is helping to identify and realize synergies in Chapter 7.

Putting a ceiling on uncertainty

To summarize this chapter so far, while buyers and sellers can draw on a number of well-established methods and metrics, no human or computer is likely to deliver the perfect price – that is, a magic figure that will instantly satisfy both parties.

Instead, the best that most parties can hope for at this stage of the dealmaking process is what we might call a 'corridor of uncertainty'. The simple human response to this corridor of uncertainty is to build a floor and a roof on it. Typically, buyers will establish a walkaway price (the 'ceiling price' beyond which the deal makes no sense because the cost of the deal will exceed the potential benefits) while the seller will set a so-called 'floor price' below which they and their owners will not be willing to part company with their business as no one wants to give away their company for less than its perceived worth.

That's not just a theory or negotiation tactic (although certainly it could be both), it is the authors' collective experience of the way deals work and, to our knowledge, always have done. Whether that's a result of basic human instinct or cultural conditioning we will leave to experts in psychology, but we would note that this approach also tends to be the starting point for some common consumer purchases such as buying a second-hand car. You set a guide price based on what similar models with the same mileage and condition generally go for but resolve to pay a little less if possible, while the car salesperson works from the opposite perspective, attempting to justify and achieve a price higher than the guide. Of course, in business dealmaking as in second-hand car sales, this all assumes that the seller's floor price isn't above the buyer's ceiling price, because then no deal will take place unless there is pressure from some other factors (such as impending bankruptcy if the company isn't sold or if the company founder just wants a quick sale in order to move onto his or her next venture or perhaps even to retire).

That may suggest that it's just the way we humans roll, even when it came to setting the barter rate for the number of sheep per cow or axe heads per wheatsheaf 3,000 years ago.

The art of the deal price

Theoretically, striking an equilibrium price between the 'ceiling price' for the bidder and the 'floor price' for the target means balancing the intrinsic value of the target (plus the added synergies and less the costs of the deal), with a figure that fairly compensates the seller for both forgoing their assets and the returns they can expect to achieve over time.

Realistically, there is currently only one way to reach this supposed equilibrium and that's through negotiation. Here we enter the classic territory of human instinct, experience, and the associated clichés beloved by filmmakers, from the smoky all-night board and conference rooms of yore to the shouty mobile phone calls of more recent fiction.

A classic case, surely, where all such interaction must be left to humans and preferably alpha types at that? Perhaps not, as we discovered in Chapter 3 when we looked at the potential of technologies such as AI, NLP and NLG (natural language generation), powered by their ability to collect and scour all manner of structured and unstructured data to add insights both before and during the negotiation process.

For those struggling to agree that technology can ever play an important part in something so essentially human as face-to-face negotiations, there is an interesting parallel with poker. In 2019, an artificial intelligence program developed by Carnegie Mellon University in collaboration with Facebook proved its worth by beating 'hands down' an assortment of top professional poker players (Carnegie Mellon University, 2019). Could this happen with the pricing negotiation in a company's sale?

Technology versus testosterone: the fight for alpha

In addition to agreeing to the general facts about the deal (such as the assets and people to be included in the transaction, future potential of the business, major risk factors, etc, all of which can be assisted by the new technologies noted earlier), in finding a common deal agreement that incorporates their respective starting positions and relative strengths, both parties generally face two difficulties during the negotiations – time pressure and psychological pressure. Hence, the success of this stage is largely dictated by the experience of the deal negotiators and advisers, which determines the level of knowledge and willingness to use psychological strategies and tactical ploys.

In fact, these methods allow negotiators to identify gamesmanship such as fake stalemates and phantom bidders, and to tackle bottlenecks in a timely manner, with the possibility of offering potential concessions to reward positive signals from the other side. As a result, interpreting body language remains an important skill at the centre of the negotiation process, but this is complicated by differences in nationality, culture and other demographic factors, not to say the increasing tendency, post-Covid, of conducting negotiations remotely by Zoom, Teams or some other online technology where the full range of physical reactions can't be observed.

> **TECHNOLOGIES APPLIED TO VALUATION AND PRICING**
>
> AI to assess behaviour
>
> There is already evidence of analytics that are able to interpret the behaviour and intention of bidders, thereby providing valuable insights to the deal team. In this respect, Australian company Ansarada's AI Bidder Engagement Score claims that the accuracy of their algorithms in analysing bidder behaviour is close to 97 per cent by day seven of a deal (Martin, 2022). With these insights, Ansarada claim that it is possible to make faster decisions in the process, with particular interest in areas such as counteroffers, risk of withdrawals, decisions about critical employees, product lines, etc. As reported by Protocol in April 2022, 'Sales and customer service software companies including Uniphore and Sybill are building products that use AI in an attempt to help humans understand and

respond to human emotion' (Kaye, 2022). Although designed for sales meetings, we can reasonably assume that these could easily be adapted for use by M&A dealmakers.

Technology to model outcomes

Management may well be interested in assessing the likelihood of other competitors joining the bidding party for the target, as well as the counteroffer value that they could propose at any point in time during the deal process, but especially following the deal announcement. Here, tools already exist that assess the likelihood of bids as well as each bidder's chances of winning in the case of bidding wars. Of course, this technology is also useful for the buyer to assess, for example, the likelihood that another bidder will enter the contest for the target.

Tools to resolve contractual difficulties

While current dealmaking tools may identify areas of concern (e.g. restrictive clauses in contracts, undisclosed operational issues, etc) via text mining and segmentation, they do not offer solutions and/or alternatives to these problems during the negotiation process. A future application of AI may therefore help to resolve these problems (e.g. indicate a more accurate deal price, propose appropriate and better contract clauses, identify the undisclosed economic risks and collect relevant data prior to the negotiations) in different ways such as, for example, 'web scraping' information on similar deals. Remember what Rob Lawson of BP said in Chapter 1 about lawyers, where he predicted that their working patterns in a deal could change as 'legal and contractual documentation has the potential for much greater automation'.

Body language

Just as poker players are famously said to have their unconscious 'tells', humans around negotiating tables may reveal more than they or their counterparties notice. AI tools already exist that can analyse areas like body language and voices of individuals in recorded and live videos. In April 2022, it was reported that Zoom was developing a system called Zoom IQ for Sales that would at some point in the future provide companies that host sales meetings not only with the conversation transcriptions but also a

> sentiment analysis (Kaye, 2022). In our understanding, these tools are not yet being commonly deployed in the actual negotiation process, possibly due to the potentially adverse reactions of those involved and/or the potential legal implications. These issues could, however, be overcome through greater transparency about their use and benefits, with all recordings made readily available for review by all the parties to the negotiation.

The future of pricing

Rob Lawson, BP's former global head of M&A, also has an interesting take on how technology could close the gap between buyer and seller price expectations. He believes that such disparities are often the result of each side using different assumptions when they calculate the price. Given the huge number of options for valuation methodologies, as outlined earlier in the chapter, this is hardly news, but Rob's suggestion is both simple and surprising. He believes that specially designed software could allow both buyer and seller to enter the assumptions and models on which their pricing is based. The technology would then compare those assumptions and identify material differences. The beauty of his 'black box' is that it would be independent, agnostic, and the input information would be kept secret so neither side would be giving away confidential information.

To support his call for this technology, Rob provides a hypothetical case where negotiations for the purchase of a wind farm are at an impasse, with a significant gap between the buyer's ceiling and the seller's floor prices, until it becomes clear through the proposed technology that the other side's valuation model is built on a higher inflation rate and set of cost assumptions for equipment. Once identified, it is easier to align price expectations, particularly if our 'black box' suggests that all the other valuation assumptions, from energy prices to wind speeds, are in the same ballpark. 'Something like that would be a breakthrough,' concludes Rob. In all likelihood, someone else somewhere has also noted this potential solution and may soon be offering it as a service to the M&A industry.

Valuing emerging technologies

As key players in BP's shift to increasingly clean energy, Rob and his team are gaining experience in the art and science of setting valuations in complex emerging technologies where valuation models are untested and comparisons difficult to make. In Chapter 1, he provided the example of when BP bought the UK's largest electric vehicle charging network, Chargemaster, for £130 million in 2018 (BBC, 2018) and then added to BP's capabilities in this field with the purchase of US-based fleet charging start-up Amply in 2021 (Hurst and Baker, 2021). Here, while drawing on data visualization tools and deep market insight to support price discovery, Rob believes that, ultimately, 'the deal valuation is what the owner is willing to sell at and so inevitably it becomes about negotiation, about connecting across the table and trying to find deal space.'

While many believe that negotiation is an art best left to humans, Martin Rand, creator of AI-powered negotiation tool Pactum, disagrees. As we heard in Chapter 3, he believes that the complexity of negotiations, driven by the sheer number of moving parts involved, means that humans compensate by taking too narrow a view, routinely leaving value on the table as a result. He also believes that humans are frequently poor negotiators, tending to focus on areas of disagreement and conflict rather than collaborating to find win-wins.

Martin does, however, outline areas where humans do excel, from cultural differences and so-called gut feeling to our ability to think laterally or, in common parlance, out of the box. Crucially, he also believes that price should be left as late as possible in the negotiation because it is likely to be a major sticking point and source of friction. 'By then, so much positive energy has been created throughout the negotiations and value expanded that it's much easier,' he explains. His vision for the future is a tool that can instantly and constantly recalculate price when underlying factors, such as commodity prices, change.

That sounds a little similar to the 'black box' that Rob Lawson was calling for in the previous section of this chapter – so, watch this space.

The song remains the same

From the evidence and anecdotes presented in this chapter, we can conclude that technology is clearly making great progress, not only into the science but also the art of pricing, as it makes ever greater inroads in understanding and predicting the human mind and human interactions. While that progress will undoubtedly continue, and hopefully go a long way towards eliminating the emotion and ego-driven mistakes outlined in Chapter 1, we concur with Rob Lawson of BP that it will still be humans who will agree the final price, finalize the deal and ultimately be held responsible for the consequences.

> **KEY POINTS**
>
> - Technology is making significant progress in helping companies better set and justify pricing.
> - But the vast range of pricing methods, assumptions and modelling available means that even the most scientifically driven pricing will always be subject to challenge and will be influenced by human factors such as emotion and competitive tension.
> - In conclusion, although human negotiation will likely always remain necessary to finalize a deal price, emerging technologies, particularly AI, will prove to be increasingly useful tools to interpret behaviours and identify pricing roadblocks.

References

Ali, A (2020) The soaring value of intangible assets in the S&P 500, *Visual Capitalist*, 12 November, www.visualcapitalist.com/the-soaring-value-of-intangible-assets-in-the-sp-500/https://www.visualcapitalist.com/the-soaring-value-of-intangible-assets-in-the-sp-500/ (archived at https://perma.cc/SL8Q-TE6J)

BBC (2018) BP buys UK's largest car charging firm Chargemaster, *BBC News*, 28 June, www.bbc.co.uk/news/business-44640647 (archived at https://perma.cc/U6F6-C7A8)

Booth, E (2022) Buffett, Lynch and Graham – how to invest like the best during uncertainty, *Hargreaves Lansdown*, 4 March, www.hl.co.uk/news/articles/buffett,-lynch-and-graham-how-to-invest-like-the-best-during-uncertainty#:~:text=Buffett%20once%20said%2C%20%E2%80%9CBen%20Graham,when%20it%20is%20marked%20down.%E2%80%9D (archived at https://perma.cc/K8NK-ERJY)

Carnegie Mellon University (2019) Carnegie Mellon and Facebook AI beats professionals in six-player poker, *Carnegie Mellon University-News*, 11 July, www.cmu.edu/news/stories/archives/2019/july/cmu-facebook-ai-beats-poker-pros.html (archived at https://perma.cc/4YKH-W526)

Deseret News (1999) U.K.'s Vodafone wins AirTouch bidding war with $56b in cash and stock, *Deseret News*, 16 January, www.deseret.com/1999/1/16/19423615/u-k-s-vodafone-wins-airtouch-bidding-war-with-56b-in-cash-and-stock (archived at https://perma.cc/75FV-CD77)

Eccles, R, Lanes, K and Wilson, T (1999) Are you paying too much for that acquisition? *Harvard Business Review*, July–August, https://hbr.org/1999/07/are-you-paying-too-much-for-that-acquisition (archived at https://perma.cc/PT7H-GJY2)

Faelten A, Driessen, M and Moeller, S (2016) *Why Deals Fail & How To Rescue Them*, The Economist in association with Profile Books Ltd and PublicAffairs, New York

Hoium, T (2021) Better buy: Tesla vs. General Motors, *The Motley Fool*, 22 January, www.fool.com/investing/2021/01/22/better-buy-tesla-vs-general-motors/ (archived at https://perma.cc/7MCJ-WKBD)

Hurst, L and Baker, D R (2021) BP expands EV charging business in U.S. with Amply power deal, *Bloomberg UK*, 7 December, www.bloomberg.com/news/articles/2021-12-07/BP-expands-ev-charging-business-in-u-s-with-amply-power-deal (archived at https://perma.cc/W9XL-WA57)

Kaye, K (2022) Companies are using AI to monitor your mood during sales calls. Zoom might be next, *Protocol*, 13 April, www.protocol.com/enterprise/emotion-ai-sales-virtual-zoom (archived at https://perma.cc/KP6M-R3BE)

Malay Mail (2014) WhatsApp to add voice calls after Facebook acquisition, *Malay Mail*, 25 February, www.malaymail.com/news/tech-gadgets/2014/02/25/whatsapp-to-add-voice-calls-after-facebook-acquisition/624457 (archived at https://perma.cc/A9Z9-XAY8)

Martin, C (2022) AiQ Bidder Engagement Score, *Ansarada*, no date, https://help.ansarada.com/en/articles/2588132-aiq-bidder-engagement-score (archived at https://perma.cc/SBW5-VK7L)

McKeever, V (2021) There's a 'unique' opportunity in art, which has beat the S&P 500 over 25 years, asset manager says, *CNBC*, 27 May, www.cnbc.com/2021/05/27/there-are-unique-opportunities-in-art-says-one-asset-manager.html (archived at https://perma.cc/6Z57-HPP8)

Pogrebin, R and Reyburn, S (2017) A Basquiat sells for 'mind-blowing' $110.5 million at auction, *The New York Times*, 18 May, www.nytimes.com/2017/05/18/arts/jean-michel-basquiat-painting-is-sold-for-110-million-at-auction.html (archived at https://perma.cc/K55H-DKKW)

Richter, W (2021) Tesla's market cap (Gigantic) v. next 10 automakers v. Tesla's global market share (minuscule), *Wolf Street*, 26 October. https://wolfstreet.com/2021/10/26/teslas-market-cap-gigantic-v-next-10-automakers-v-teslas-global-market-share-minuscule/ (archived at https://perma.cc/88ZW-VZ6C)

Ritchie, G (2022) JPMorgan product reveals Wall Street's shifting views on ESG, *Bloomberg*, 7 September, www.bloomberg.com/news/articles/2022-09-07/jpmorgan-product-reveals-wall-street-s-shifting-views-on-esg (archived at https://perma.cc/29ZH-S8Z9)

Suria, A (2021) Airbnb: worth more than Marriott, Hilton and Hyatt combined, *Seeking Alpha*, 11 November, https://seekingalpha.com/article/4468431-airbnb-worth-more-than-marriott-hilton-and-hyatt-combined (archived at https://perma.cc/EN4E-6T2W)

Villa, A (2021) The most expensive Jean-Michel Basquiat works ever sold at auction, *ART News*, 8 March, www.artnews.com/list/art-news/artists/jean-michel-basquiat-most-expensive-works-1234585981/jean-michel-basquiat-flesh-and-spirit-1982-1983/ (archived at https://perma.cc/W29Z-37U3)

5

Taking care of business

*More data and new technologies are helping
due diligence to keep pace with a changing deal world,
but human judgement remains vital.*

Big deals create headlines. One classic example is Kraft's £11.5 billion acquisition of UK confectionery company Cadbury in 2010 (RTÉ, 2010). It's the story of a powerful overseas buyer bidding to take over a famous national institution in a country with a notoriously sweet tooth. A combination that meant the deal stayed on the newspaper front pages from when the deal first was publicized in September 2009 until well after it was agreed in January 2010.

But one aspect of any deal story that rarely triggers the interest of the press is due diligence. For the uninformed reader that makes perfect sense. The very words 'due diligence' may suggest a dull formality in dusty rooms. Yet, as we'll examine, due diligence was so key to the Kraft/Cadbury deal that it led to far-reaching changes well beyond that particular deal and has impacted how transactions are done today. To bring us bang up to date, we'll also be talking to an experienced senior transaction executive who has carried out the sale, acquisition and IPO of multibillion-dollar businesses, where all due diligence was done online. Plus, we'll get the views of the innovators and technologists who are breaking new ground in this area.

But first, let's talk about our definitions. Broadly speaking, due diligence is a crucial process in every deal because it enables the buyer to verify the true nature and value of the target, as well as providing the target company with clarity over the buyer's finances and intentions.

What can go wrong will go wrong: when due diligence fails

History is littered with cases of even the biggest, most reputable and best-run companies making what appeared to be elementary due diligence errors. One famous historic example was Volkswagen's £430 million bid for Rolls-Royce's automotive business in 1998 (Fleet News, 1998). Only after the bid was accepted did Volkswagen discover that the iconic Rolls-Royce marque was not included as part of the deal. So, despite paying what would now be well over £1 billion in today's money, Volkswagen did not have the right to produce a single Rolls-Royce vehicle (The Herald, 1998).

The point of the quick history lesson is that if mistakes like that could happen in the relatively simple and straightforward business world of the late 20th century, where does that leave us now? Remember how a consistent theme in Chapters 1 and 2 was the increasing need for companies to do more deals at greater speed and with greater complexity, including increasingly across borders? Often, this entails companies venturing beyond their own sectors to acquire the (often new) capabilities that they need to stay relevant in markets that are being disrupted at pace by new players and technologies.

We will go on to look at these challenges in more detail but it should already be apparent that they make due diligence both more necessary and harder to perform. To illustrate how due diligence has become more complex, let's take the fictional example of a UK regional paint manufacturer. Back in 2000, it bids for its competitor on the other side of town. As it will probably already know a lot, not only about the target but also about its customers and suppliers, due diligence will most likely focus on any 'skeletons in the cupboard' that could lead to the acquirer inadvertently taking on unseen liabilities, from debt to pensions, or hidden costs such as generous severance terms for senior executives. The biggest complication is likely to be that, as a close competitor, the target company will be reluctant to share anything before the deal closes that they don't absolutely have to disclose. Later on in this chapter we'll see how due diligence becomes more challenging in today's world for our fictional paint manufacturer as it is forced to step out of its comfort zone to keep up to speed with new and changing markets.

Know the rules: regulation and due diligence

It's important to remember that takeovers in particular, and indeed most areas of modern-day business, are subject to strict regulation. We don't intend to go into great detail on this particular subject (and strongly recommend that anyone doing a deal makes sure that there's a very good lawyer on the deal team) but, broadly speaking, such regulation must be a key consideration during due diligence. Any deal must comply with M&A rules and regulations (often competition-related), plus having a proper understanding of any legislation applying to a target company's operations will be essential when carrying out due diligence. To take a simple example, if strict labour laws prevent the acquirer from slimming down or even reskilling the target company's workforce, then the assumed synergies that drove the deal in the first place will be harder to achieve and may well call the entire deal's financial rationale into question.

To return to the Kraft/Cadbury case, it's interesting to note that deals can become the spur for regulation as well as the subject of it. Having made a commitment during the very public deal negotiations to keep Cadbury's Somerdale factory in Somerset open, Kraft rapidly reversed that decision after the takeover, resulting in many job losses and damaging press headlines. Kraft's defence was that Cadbury's failure to fully disclose that it already had plans in place to close the plant made it unrealistic to reverse them (Macnamara, 2010). Under the rules at the time, Cadbury was not required to provide Kraft with any non-public information about itself. However, public outrage about the post-deal job losses, combined with more general concerns within Parliament about prized UK assets and jobs being lost to aggressive, often foreign, corporates led the UK to review the existing regulations related to mergers and acquisitions. As a result, changes were made to the UK's Takeover Code, requiring more information from bidders about their intentions after the purchase, particularly in relation to job cuts, but also related to any promises that acquirers make during the deal process (Fairfield, 2014).

Disruption and the age of due diligence

Returning to the tale of our fictional, acquisitional UK paint company as it faces new challenges. In a desire to keep up to date with consumer trends, the company is now trying to acquire a US start-up firm with software that allows customers to point their phone camera at a colour they like and instantly order paint that matches it.

Typically, the due diligence challenges will be significantly greater than if it was (as previously noted) simply buying its local rival. This new deal not only has cross-border elements but also the need to assess the true efficacy of the technology and the people behind it. The risks are likely to be higher too. If you pay too much for the local paint manufacturer you will at least have taken out a competitor and will likely be left with some tangible assets such as paint stock, some real estate and factory equipment. But if you buy the wrong technology or one that is out of date quickly, you may be left with nothing to show for the time spent on the acquisition and the expense of buying that company.

That highlights a broader point about how the value, or sometimes value-destructive, nature of technology is an increasingly important part of due diligence. Areas of focus might range from the risks associated with large-scale IT projects or a particularly valuable piece of intellectual property such as proprietary software, to vulnerabilities around data privacy or cyber security.

Due diligence processes should also be looking for the upside of technology – untapped digital value that can be realized beyond the deal. For example, a smaller target company may have a much better IT environment or superiority in a specific area such as a CRM platform or quality management system that can then be leveraged across the whole organization post-merger.

Going back to our paint company one last time, speed is also a critical factor. Leave your potentially game-changing paint technology acquisition too long and the chance to stay ahead of competitors and meet the growing expectations of customers will be gone. The target may also have been purchased by another paint company while you delayed. Tarry a little when buying the local paint plant and your target is less likely to go elsewhere.

The need for speed and the value of going slow

So, as we've just outlined, proper due diligence is ever more vital but, at the same time, the pressure to get it done quickly is also growing. That tension is highlighted by some interesting and contrasting research.

A study by Bayes Business School's M&A Research Centre in London and global technology provider SS&C Intralinks found a clear relationship between longer due diligence and greater deal success (M&A Research Centre at Bayes Business School and Intralinks, 2013). The ground-breaking 2013 research found that shareholder returns for acquirers were significantly higher when the due diligence process took longer. In fact, acquirers outperformed the market by 18.8 per cent when they had a longer than average due diligence period, compared with an underperformance of 6.7 per cent for acquirees involved in deals with a shorter due diligence period.

Yet, research conducted in 2021 by professional services firm Accenture revealed that moving too slowly can also have a cost (Albert et al, 2021). It found that, for a $1 billion revenue business sold at the median industry EBITDA multiple, being able to complete a transaction three months earlier could generate significant value: up to $15–$30 million for the buyer and $15–$45 million for the seller.

> **BIDDING BY TWEET: THE DEAL AT WARP SPEED**
>
> The pluses and perils of acting quickly when making an acquisition were exemplified by Elon Musk's 2022 $44 billion bid for Twitter. While Musk's innate ability to act fast put him ahead of any potential competitor in launching a bid for the San Francisco-based company, it also caused problems. Quoted on forbes.com, George Geis, a corporate law professor at the University of Virginia, explained that 'Most merger agreements do have an obligation on the sellers' part to assist the buyer with due diligence. But Musk waived that' (Brown, 2022). Having concerns that there were many more bots on Twitter than the company acknowledged, Musk sought to renegotiate or terminate the deal, while Twitter sought to hold him to his original offer. The deal made headlines around the world for many reasons, but one lesson is the importance of due diligence and how even the most fleet-footed and well-funded bidder will be impacted by it sooner or later.

More haste, more speed: using technology to square the circle

So, how are today's companies and their advisers managing to square this particular circle? How can more complex due diligence be carried out more effectively across more borders, sectors, products, services and capabilities, more quickly, and achieve the benefits and value that were anticipated and expected? Attentive readers will not be at all surprised to hear that this is once again an area where deal-related technology is riding to the rescue.

Before we look at those technologies and how they are being used in practice, it is worth noting that this is happening within the context of due diligence having moved from a more traditional box-ticking exercise to something more dynamic and interactive, with greater relevance throughout the deal process. This is focused more and more on the value drivers and value opportunities and often extends well beyond the traditional synergies expected from putting two similar companies together.

Due diligence adds value during the deal cycle

There are a couple of elements to this story that are worth exploring in more detail. In the past, due diligence was often a narrower and more strictly controlled process. Some readers – and at least one of our authors – will remember when doing due diligence required a trip to the lawyer's office. There the seller had deposited the relevant boxes of paper documents in dusty cardboard file boxes, piled high upon each other in a basement storage room. There was often no apparent organization to those files, thus requiring the due diligence team to spend hours upon hours literally leafing through the papers to determine if there was anything of relevance contained therein. Throughout that process, a watchful attendant (typically a paralegal) would carefully note exactly which documents had been examined, for how long and by whom. If the due diligence was part of a sell-side auction process, each team would be given a slot of time to access those boxes. If the bid was hostile, no data room would be provided at all or, if one had to be in place for regulatory reasons, it could turn out to be as much about obfuscation as discovery. In such circumstances, where the target is under no obligation to provide information to its would-be acquirer, the only option is to seek out publicly available information, from annual reports and news articles to seeking the views of ex-employees, competitors and industry experts.

Fortunately, the world has moved beyond paper. Proprietary corporate information is now available online, albeit often beyond a firewall. Public information can also be found in almost limitless quantities online. With such data sources digitized and searchable, along with others we'll come to later, it's altogether easier to find information and less worthwhile trying to hide it.

Coupled with this added access is the increasing desire to use the knowledge acquired during due diligence more effectively throughout the deal process, from gaining investor confidence to anticipating, identifying and addressing problems at the contractual and transactional stages of deal execution. As we discussed in Chapter 3, so-called vendor due diligence can be a way of getting more out of buyers during the negotiation or auction process – if the seller provides the information that will satisfy buyers, they may tempt more of them and to pay more. But it is at the post-deal stage that such information can be most valuable. Those early disclosures and discoveries can play a key part in not only identifying the synergies that may be created after the deal is done but also how they can then be realized.

How the Covid-19 pandemic changed due diligence

One widely recognized impact of the Covid-19 pandemic was the forced adaptation of technology in everyday business life, and dealmaking was no exception. While the lack of human interaction and relationship building presented some barriers, perhaps favouring those deals where some of that initial courting and trust building had already been done pre-pandemic, the actual deal process, and specifically due diligence, benefited from the move to fully digital. Because travel was largely prohibited and impossible, no journey time was needed before due diligence sessions. A greater audience of decision makers was often possible through virtual meetings or by pre-recording a management presentation, which was then distributed to all potential buyers.

As the authors pondered on the learnings from this extraordinary period, one conclusion must certainly be that a number of myths associated with dealmaking were well and truly busted. One such myth was that a buyer can't invest in a company without having met the founders in person, the so-called 'look them in the eye' hurdle. Or that proper due diligence cannot be completed without having on-site visits and 'kicking the tyres'. All of this was disproven many times over during the pandemic; our key interviewee in Chapter 1, Rob Lawson of BP, told us about a $5 billion deal that they did early in the pandemic where the parties never met physically.

Driving synergies, even at the due diligence stage

With price multiples hitting new highs in the early 2020s, the need to better understand and realize synergies, in order to justify those high price multiples, has grown. It's also increasingly a technology issue, because the compatibility (or lack of it) between target and acquirer IT systems will likely impact post-deal synergies. The added focus on business transformation, generally a shorthand for using digitization to improve the operating model, is often part of the post-deal strategy and will also likely depend on the quality and compatibility of technology. This adds pressure to use the due diligence process more actively to thoroughly understand the potential synergies and, just as

Taking new factors into account during due diligence

If the authors were still in the unfortunate position of having to physically sift through information, then the law firm mentioned earlier hosting the due diligence data room may well need larger offices, or even a warehouse. That's because, as the business world has evolved, not only has the volume of data produced expanded exponentially, but we have also developed what we could call a more rounded or holistic view of companies. As a consequence, while due diligence was once almost exclusively about financial matters – such as verifying legal documents with clients and suppliers, company trading accounts, tax statements and the corporate balance sheet – the remit has now spread further (see Figure 5.1). So-called 'soft factors', such as the culture of an organization or its carbon footprint, diversity and its relationship with its local community, must all be taken into account while conducting due diligence.

FIGURE 5.1 Overview of 'hard and soft' due diligence factors

Soft factors, hard landings: taking a more rounded view

To find out more about the cultural aspect of due diligence, we talked to Adrian Moorhouse, who founded Lane4 Management Group, a UK talent development, organizational performance and culture change consultancy, in 1995. But he may be more familiar to some UK readers as the Olympic gold-winning breaststroke swimmer who topped the podium in Seoul in 1998.

Adrian's company has a lot of experience helping people work better together post-deal, so we'll hear a lot more from him in Chapter 7, but he also has an interesting view on how, even if the fit between acquirer and target makes perfect economic sense, culture must also be taken into account during due diligence. That's because he believes it represents a 'significantly strong barrier that deserves to be thoughtfully investigated'. Having helped with the post-merger integration of cost-conscious, process-driven cellular network T-Mobile and its brand-led, more flamboyant rival Orange in 2010, he knows that similar cultures can fit together more quickly and less expensively while clashing cultures take more time and money to fix, as well as creating greater risks that key talent may leave.

Given this book's hypothesis, it's interesting to note that Adrian believes technology is now playing a greater role in evaluating culture, with a number of tools available to help, albeit usually requiring some human input, from focus groups to filling out survey forms. But it's clear that careful and close examination is required: 'You need to understand the espoused culture, the lived culture and the deep culture,' Adrian adds, meaning that due diligence must go beyond what people say about culture to what is really under the skin.

Staying onside with stakeholders

Similarly, there are numerous examples where companies' disregard of their environment, employees, customers or local communities has not only damaged those stakeholders but also led to financial penalties and/or loss of shareholder value. For example, so-called 'fast fashion' firms have seen share prices plunge as the behaviour of their low-cost suppliers has been exposed, energy companies have received huge financial penalties for environmental damage, and leading tech companies have been hit by allegations of sexist working practices.

So, this is yet another set of factors that must be taken into account and they are making due diligence more complex than ever before. Research findings by Datasite, a platform that works across the M&A life cycle, in 2020 show that ESG and other non-traditional elements of due diligence are now firmly in the deal picture, with 88 per cent of respondents saying that deals have not progressed due to concerns about a target company's ESG credentials (Datasite, 2020).

The role of technology in due diligence

Stage one: closing the information gap

As our next interviewee for this chapter, Ashish Agarwal, former senior vice president, strategy and corporate development at global computer security software company McAfee, puts it, 'The information gap has been closed'. The gap he is referring to is that, historically, the biggest disadvantage facing a would-be buyer was lack of access, without specialist help or seller disclosure, to even fairly basic information about the target company. Thanks to search engines and software that can scour documents in seconds that gap has largely been closed.

Stage two: moving out of the data room

As those physical data rooms full of paper are moved online, the ability to search, interrogate, model and glean insight from that data becomes fast and easy. We'll talk to a data analyst about the technology in more detail shortly, but Ashish's long career overseeing multibillion-dollar transactions means he can give us a privileged overview of the rapidly changing landscape. He explains how this initial shift 'made the diligence process more efficient. We didn't need to have to do multiple things – we didn't need to go to meetings in lawyers' offices with multiple investors and buyers while managing data and documents – we could just do it virtually and in parallel.'

The huge deals that Ashish has recently overseen qualify him as a significant contributor to this debate. In November 2021 he sold his company McAfee to a PE consortium comprising Advent, Permira, Crosspoint Capital, CPP Investments, GIC and ADIA for $14 billion (representing a 22.6 per cent premium), with the entire transaction carried out online.

A few months prior to that, in March 2021, he oversaw the sale of McAfee's Enterprise Business to PE company Symphony Technology Group for $4 billion and again the transaction was completed entirely online with no person-to-person meetings. And prior to that he took the company public in a $740 million IPO done virtually. 'I used to be a banker in a prior life, doing investor meetings from city to city for IPOs. For McAfee's IPO my CEO and I did all the investor meetings virtually. Every single investor meeting was done by online video calls,' he explains.

So, in summary: IPO, divestiture and the sale of the company – not only was all due diligence conducted online but also every aspect of the three deals.

Did due diligence start the virtual deal revolution?

Ashish's account of the gradual encroachment of technology into the deal process, from data rooms and due diligence all the way to execution and beyond, sounds like less of a digital transformation and more like plain old common sense. He explains: 'We didn't have to deal with NYC traffic. We didn't need to deal with airports and fly for one meeting. It also allowed us to be more confidential in our dealings. We didn't have to explain why the head of strategy and CEO were disappearing for half a day of meetings, we could just do it online, and it maintained our confidentiality as we could have meetings with multiple buyers or investors.'

It also sparks an interesting hypothesis (and just to clarify, this is the authors' own conjecture, not Ashish's). Put simply, did the march towards online, technology-tooled deal processes actually begin with due diligence? Were virtual data rooms the first step in the broader shift of deal processes online? Was due diligence the spark that started the online fire?

The basis for this conjecture is that, if we go back to the days when the information gap existed, perhaps it created the perception that, with so many unknowns, the only way to find 'the truth' was to look the person in the eye and watch them blink (or not) as you asked them tough but critical questions. In other words, the need for human physical connection was driven by that lack of information, or what we might now call data. Once data became plentifully available and relatively easy to access, the pressure on the physical connection lessened, paving the way for technology to establish itself throughout the deal process, turbo charged of course by the Covid-19 pandemic, which required remote working and virtual meetings.

The importance of human connection

Ashish quickly throws a wrench in the gears of this particular argument, however, stopping us right in our tracks. Despite being an enthusiastic adopter of technology, he remains fully committed to the importance of human interaction.

'At the end of the day, that meeting, whether it be virtual or in person, is still a critical decision-making point. I don't think that's going to go away. It's not about looking someone in the eye, it's actually about understanding a point of view. "Why should I buy your company or invest in your company? Help me understand." That conviction doesn't come without having a conversation, whether that conversation be on video or over the phone or in person,' says Ashish.

While recognizing that the nature of his business as an online software provider made it easier and quicker to adopt deal technology, he believes that there is no fundamental reason why other, less tech-focused sectors could not take the same approach. 'I think the difference is just in the adoption curve,' Ashish concludes.

Unlocking the potential of technology

As you might expect of someone who spends his working life helping companies to use data and technology to gain advantage throughout the deal process, Tony Qui (who featured in Chapter 2) sees widespread potential in improving due diligence, not only to save time but also to create better insights, whether that be to mitigate risks or improve opportunities.

Yet, at present, he sees a lot of that potential going untapped.

Tony explains: 'In terms of using AI or machine learning to extract insights, I would say the industry as a whole is still at the early stages. It's still quite passive information gathering: you put it in a virtual data room and what you actually do with it is still very manual. I haven't seen a predictive or proactive part of it yet, or how would that work or how that would evolve.'

> **TECH TALK: A BRIEF SUMMARY OF KEY APPLICATIONS**
>
> Let's take a moment here to summarize the impact and application of key technologies that will disrupt due diligence.
>
> Predictive analytics and AI will, when used well, not only make better, faster predictions of future financial and operational performance, but also identify how those predictions are made and why. The how and why are key, because ultimately due diligence is a risk-based view we give about the appropriateness (or otherwise) of a future business plan, so being able to do that better, more quickly, with a better understanding of risk is key. These predictions will be assessed against those of the management team and will help challenge or support the business plan.
>
> NLP will also impact diligence as it will identify and then 'read' documents at huge volumes and speed to identify key themes/issues of interest. This is still, ultimately, an analysis of the historic past. It is the future predictive capabilities of technology that will perhaps be the real disruptor for due diligence. There is more on those at the end of this chapter and in our interview with Steve King of Black Swan Data in Chapter 2.

Barriers to adoption: formats and risk

Tony Qui identifies one of the barriers to using more advanced technologies as the number of different formats within the data rooms that drive due diligence.

'You could have an Excel spreadsheet, a PDF, a word document, or an image. With multiple different document types, it is very hard to reconcile pieces of information together to give you one insight. If you look at most of the machine learning use cases you see that the format of the information is quite static,' he continues.

The challenge ahead is not only to mature the technology to cope better with multiple formats but also the legalities. If, for example, a machine learning model extracts crucial due diligence information which then proves to be faulty, who will be held liable in a deal process that can often be highly litigious with disgruntled employees, suppliers, customers and shareholders?

It's worth adding here that although Tony's focus is on the barriers specific to effective data use, there are broader obstacles to overcome. These include the hesitation of some dealmakers to embrace technology during the due diligence process, whether due to a lack of relevant technology skills or the desire to 'do things as they have always been done'. Time pressure is also often cited by deal professionals who, with the clock ticking, feel they don't have the time to learn new skills. In our concluding chapter, *The future of the deal*, we look at how technology can overcome these challenges through better alignment with the specific needs of dealmakers and by becoming more intuitive and user friendly.

Creating better models

In the specific areas highlighted by Tony, however, he is positive that progress is already being made. 'With more and more virtual data rooms and people keeping data longer, there's the possibility for us to train the models better.'

In this context, he means a model, based on learning from previous data sets, that can then be applied to other datasets to extract the required insights or predictions. This can be adapted to meet the needs of an individual acquiring company or an investor, such as a specific hedge fund or private equity house. In a world of accessible technology, there is no longer a need for 'one-size-fits-all', as the prediction about the ultimate success of a deal will differ according to the buyer.

This positive must be measured against another issue that needs to be navigated. Typically, data rooms are facilitated by third-party providers, who do not actually own the data, which remains the possession of the sell-side company. So the buyer may not be able to get consent to access the data required to train their model. An echo back, perhaps, to those watchful lawyers dutifully controlling and monitoring access to information in dusty offices. In time, this may be solved by using metadata, but we're not there yet.

However, if time has taught us anything, it's that the barriers to technology adoption rarely last long and Tony believes that there are already big advances being made. 'I think the big game changer in diligence is actually getting supplementary information outside of your data room: benchmarking, pricing, market information and customer sentiments,' he explains. One example of a benchmarking tool embedded in the diligence process is EY Diligence Edge. This not only provides a virtual data room by ingesting the hundreds or thousands of documents available and making them searchable, it also creates an outside-in view of a target company and its competitors by consolidating and analysing a range of external information, including news, financial and social media data.

The inside track on data: a view from the virtual coal face

So far, we have only talked to people at the top of the tree. Those with a big-picture view of how data is reshaping due diligence and whether it is replacing or re-arming human perspectives. But what about those at the coal face, or should that be computer screen, whose job it is to actually marshal and manage the data itself? To get that perspective we sought the view of a number of experienced data analysts who have been involved in due diligence.

Interestingly, they believe that the two most heavily touted areas of technology-led improvement in due diligence have not yet been realized. The ability of software to automate the extraction of information from the data room to, for example, fill templates during the due diligence process has been frustrated by the factors that Tony Qui mentioned earlier, such as different file formats. Currently, they explain, the only way around this is often by reverting to manual interaction. They believe that, despite the many new smart software tools and technologies available, the real driver of change is simply the increase in computational power, making the processing of information so much faster.

They do, however, believe that the scope of due diligence has broadened and explain how they are now doing diligence on topics that they did not before. They provide two examples to support their argument, which deserve further exploration.

Added due diligence on technology

In a business world where, as we've established throughout this book, technology has huge value, it's understandable that effective due diligence must consider its useful lifespan as well as current value. One data expert recalls that when carrying out due diligence on an acquisition in the home security market, they helped the buyer to understand the technology landscape they were entering into. To provide context, this was at a time when the managed home security market, essentially wired burglary prevention systems supported by a call centre, was in the process of being replaced by what we're all now used to, namely wireless devices producing cloud-based data that can easily be accessed remotely on standard mobile devices.

The crucial point here is that, without any expert industry knowledge or opinion, our data analyst was able to collect enough data to model the trajectory for new technology adoption, supported by wider knowledge drawn from established thinking such as the Bass Diffusion model, which outlines how technology comes into the market following an 'S curve' (Nielsen, 1995). As time has passed, this prediction of technology adoption within the home security market has been proven to be extremely accurate and is clearly a valuable element of due diligence that would prove fundamental to the buying decision.

While there is little doubt that the human ability to access the right data and ask it the right questions was crucial, the human expert/opinion element, often essential in making such predictions and nuanced calls, was absent – and without any detriment. Does this signal that at least some areas of human expertise have been devalued by data?

Due diligence, ESG and the end of the expert

In the lead-up to the UK's referendum on membership of the European Union in 2016, MP and cabinet member Michael Gove touched a nerve with his widely reported comment, 'I think the people of this country have had enough of experts' (Portes, 2017). Yet, this controversial view also finds an unlikely parallel in the calmer seas of due diligence. One data analyst explains that, in such circumstances, expert human opinion is not only unnecessary but can actually be a liability, as it is just one person's opinion yet can sometimes be taken as 'gospel' truth without proper examination.

The analysts also highlighted the ESG factors that are becoming increasingly important when a target's credentials are being assessed. They explain that this means, in effect, hoovering up all the data points around what customers are saying, what society is saying and what investors are saying around ESG topics. Again, the expert view is devalued because there's enough data in the public domain to get the information needed, rather than needing to seek out the views of an ESG expert.

One data analyst then describes a similar shift away from survey-based opinions – which can be expensive, time-consuming and with built-in biases – to hard data based on actual behaviours.

So, does that lack of a need for human experts extend more broadly into due diligence? In one way, the huge growth in 'aggregators' that pick up data and use some form of machine learning to crunch it suggests that automation is not only increasingly possible but is actively being applied.

Yet that does not mean an end to human expertise and ingenuity. In fact, the more we hear about the 'tricks of the trade' in terms of how those tools are used and how dealmakers and data analysts really get under the bonnet to tweak their performance, the clearer it becomes that this is an art as well as science, requiring a human touch and expert view.

STATED AND INFERRED BEHAVIOURS

Data analysts differentiate between stated behaviours found within data, such as a target company's customer writing a bad review or making a complaint, and inferred behaviours. The latter is, according to one data analyst we spoke to, 'When you come across a number of data points and start to stitch them together to tell a story which you wouldn't otherwise know.' A simple example might be data showing an increase in web traffic to a retailer's website. By connecting this to a celebrity endorsement, the launch of a new product or a news item, valuable insight into sales drivers can be gleaned. Without the tools to find and process huge amounts of data, those inferences could not be made, but, importantly, a human sense check is still needed to make sure that the inference is credible.

Due diligence in a post-truth world

The value of human ingenuity and common sense, even in the most data-driven areas of dealmaking, is revealed in a final and telling discovery. Companies, or rather the individuals who run and work for them, are becoming increasingly canny about the data they produce and, crucially, how it will be perceived.

One data analyst noticed that sometimes before a company comes onto the market there is a spike in how much they or key stakeholders post positively about the company and its services on social media. The analyst believes that this is an attempt to directly influence the data gathered by any potential bidder, likening it to the controversy over false and/or paid for customer reviews.

In many ways, this is a direct result of the ever-broadening focus of due diligence. While very few firms would seek to give their financials an 'extreme makeover', it seems to be easier to do so with an area like customer sentiment, particularly if you know which type of data your potential acquirer will be focusing on.

With a vigilant data analyst on the case, perpetrators can be spotted, but that will not always be the case. One data analyst explained that, while running an initial due diligence sweep on a facilities provider, they found 77,000 data points. At that sort of volume, it is impossible to check them all for veracity. The current solution to that issue is sampling to make sure at least some of the data points are fully tested, but with improved information processing power and tools, better checks are being developed.

Such is their faith in the future that one data analyst even holds out hope for a fact-checking algorithm being introduced to not only highlight faulty data but also to help identify and verify true facts from false ones. Good luck with that one, as the saying goes. After all, would our inbuilt human biases allow us to accept 'the truth' even when it's scientifically verified by smart technology? And, given what our technologist has already told us about the caution with which data should be treated, even if we trusted the algorithm, could we rely on the data it was being fed?

The evolving role of key technologies in due diligence

Our experts see three key basic developments:

- Greater computational power – enabling the faster processing of huge volumes of datasets so that, for example, tools can search and score millions of social media posts.
- More sophistication – continuing to refine the way that machine learning analyses data. For example, ranging from a relatively simple identification of the target's name within written text and ascribing a simple overall score relating to the number of mentions, to doing a more precise positive/negative weighting for the words surrounding the target name.

- Making greater use of non-text sources – enabling, for example, the transcription of podcasts, video soundtracks and radio broadcasts in order to uncover facts and track trends and sentiment, then combined with AI to analyse those transcriptions.

And there is one more innovative improvement that is likely to gain further traction:

- Sometimes referred to as 'the internet of concepts', this approach allows a more flexible way of thinking about and using information. Essentially it mirrors the way we as humans connect up information, but with the power of advanced computing. One company exploring this particular area is Diffbot, a US-based developer extracting data from web pages to create a knowledge base (Maithani, 2020). It was the first company funded by StartX, Stanford University's on-campus venture capital fund. According to the Diffbot website: 'The world's largest compendium of human knowledge is buried in the code of 1.2 billion public websites. Diffbot reads it all like a human, then transforms it into usable data.'

Due diligence leads the way in terms of deal technology

Given our earlier conjecture that the birth of deal technology took place in the data room, it is hardly surprising that many see due diligence as the biggest area for future technology adoption and automation. Datasite's 2020 research on The New State of M&A revealed that UK and EMEA practitioners in particular believe that due diligence is the area of dealmaking that could be enhanced most by new technologies and digitization over the next five years (Datasite, 2020). They place greatest hope in AI and machine learning technologies, especially as part of virtual data rooms, to speed up the due diligence process.

Summing up

The two key drivers for due diligence technology are the need for speed in the form of greater automation and the desire to gain greater insight into target companies and their true value. Both are being satisfied by the combination of ever greater data sources and ever more powerful software, but these are not sufficient by themselves.

It is rather the chance to capitalize on these capabilities throughout the deal cycle that is particularly exciting for dealmakers. Not least because this gets to the heart of an increasing preoccupation around deals. As Tony Qui puts it, 'Dealmakers no longer want to merely execute the deal to completion, they want to make sure that the deal enables a transformation to take place in the company.' So, rather than a traditional and limited box-ticking process, due diligence is becoming a key stage in understanding the full potential of not just the deal itself, but what lies beyond it – an area we will explore in more detail in Chapter 7.

KEY POINTS

- Due diligence is a critical process that extends beyond risk mitigation to inform and empower the whole deal process.
- Technology is providing more than just an improvement in the efficiency and speed of the due diligence process; it can serve to unlock new insights and reveal a more complete picture of a target company's current and even future performance.
- Due diligence technology is enabling dealmakers to keep pace in a world where acquirers must act faster and venture beyond their comfort zones in terms of geography and sectors.
- Rather than replacing humans in the due diligence process, data-driven technology is empowering them to gain understanding and advantage.
- Ultimately though, no matter how thorough the due diligence, the decision to buy or not buy a target will always remain a human one, driven by trust and relationships as well as facts and data.

References

Albert, G, Chalfont, C, Duarte, G and Krimpmann, D (2021) *Accenture.com*, www.accenture.com/_acnmedia/PDF-143/Accenture-Strategy-Sweetening-Deal-Digitizing-MandA-POV.pdf (archived at https://perma.cc/9UVM-KTND)

Brown, A (2022) Elon Musk's Twitter deal has become a multibillion-dollar game of chicken, *Forbes*, 7 June, www.forbes.com/sites/abrambrown/2022/06/07/elon-musk-twitter-buyout-takeover-bots-purchase-acquisition-spam/?sh=2c27cc5d72ee (archived at https://perma.cc/X3XJ-PAZH)

Datasite (2020) The New State of M&A 2020–2025, www.datasite.com/us/en/resources/insights/reports/the-new-state-of-m-a-hub.html (archived at https://perma.cc/2E7S-2J26)

Fairfield, G (2014) Statements of intention under the UK Takeover Code – say what you mean and do what you say, Herbert Smith Freehills, 28 November, www.herbertsmithfreehills.com/latest-thinking/statements-of-intention-under-the-uk-takeover-code-%E2%80%93-say-what-you-mean-and-do-what#:~:text=Summary,as%20part%20of%20an%20offer (archived at https://perma.cc/9F4H-Q2YH)

Fleet News (1998) Volkswagen wins battle to buy Rolls-Royce, *Fleet News*, 12 June, www.fleetnews.co.uk/news/1998/6/12/volkswagen-wins-battle-to-buy-rolls-royce/3460/ (archived at https://perma.cc/77GH-DPEP)

The Herald (1998) Ecstasy agony for Volkswagen as rival secures rights to prestigious Rolls-Royce marque BMW wins name game, *The Herald*, 29 July, www.heraldscotland.com/news/12253499.ecstasy-agony-for-volkswagen-as-rival-secures-rights-to-prestigious-rolls-royce-marque-bmw-wins-name-game/ (archived at https://perma.cc/VZ4T-VCB9)

M&A Research Centre at Bayes Business School and Intralinks (2013) When no one knows Pre-announcement M&A activity and its effect on M&A outcomes, www.intralinks.com/sites/default/files/file_attach/when-no-one-knows-report.pdf (archived at https://perma.cc/6RJ8-QRRT)

Macnamara, K (2010) Kraft reverses pledge to keep Cadbury factory open, *The Independent*, 9 February, www.independent.co.uk/news/business/news/kraft-reverses-pledge-to-keep-cadbury-factory-open-1894250.html (archived at https://perma.cc/SQC6-XD6C)

Maithani, M (2020) Guide to Diffbot: multi-functional web scraper, *Analytics India Magazine*, 8 December, https://analyticsindiamag.com/diffbot/ (archived at https://perma.cc/88UT-DKZZ)

Nielsen, J (1995) Bass curves for the diffusion of innovations, *Nielsen Norman Group*, 1 September, www.nngroup.com/articles/bass-curves-for-the-diffusion-innovations/ (archived at https://perma.cc/FPX3-HJX2)

Portes, R (2017) 'I think the people of this country have had quite enough of experts', *London Business School*, 9 May, www.london.edu/think/who-needs-experts/ (archived at https://perma.cc/LR7N-SHDS)

RTÉ (2010) Cadbury agrees to £11.5 billion Kraft deal, *RTÉ*, 19 Jan, www.rte.ie/news/business/2010/0119/126514-cadbury/ (archived at https://perma.cc/CAX3-Q6YA)

6

Selling the story

Good communication is crucial to deal success, but today's multichannel world makes it increasingly hard to control the narrative

It's often said that a good CEO also needs to be a good storyteller. That doesn't mean being great at getting the kids off to sleep every night with a fairy tale or having a side project as a bestselling novelist. It's a recognition that, at heart, even the most experienced and intelligent among us prefer to hear a simple, engaging message delivered by someone that we trust.

Never is that quality more important than in the deal process. Yesterday, a company was employing its loyal people to produce established products that it sold profitably to familiar customers. Today, it says it's going to buy another business that makes something else in a different country and sells to a whole new set of people. Almost in unison, you can hear employees, customers and investors saying (and this is the polite version), 'Whaaaaat?'.

Faced with this initial response, a good CEO doesn't turn to their spreadsheet or even the security team; they reach for their story. The simplified, fairy tale version might be, 'Once upon a time there were two very different companies, but then they realized they could help each other become better together and live happily ever after.' Daft, fictional and slightly icky though that undoubtedly is, it's still strangely soothing. It is also surprisingly similar to the real thing, as demonstrated by this extract from Microsoft CEO Satya Nadella's email to employees on their 2016 acquisition of LinkedIn: 'We both care deeply about individual and collective growth, and find deep meaning in the work we do to make a difference in our world. Together we'll do just that' (Nadella, 2016).

Of course, that's just one small extract from a longer letter that clearly communicates the deal rationale and tries to carefully allay employee concerns while also setting out in detail the future plans that lie ahead, highlighting another ingredient of storytelling that is highly relevant to the deal process. Any good story has a clear ending but also leaves the reader with a preview of how the future will pan out for the protagonist. Hence the classic, if hackneyed, phrase, 'happy ever after'. So, bear in mind that while a lot of the communication and storytelling aspects in a deal will focus on its earlier stages from the initial announcement to signing on the dotted line, the real pay-off – successful integration with all the associated synergies – comes later. As we explain in the next chapter, the deal integration phase is both the most valuable and the toughest of all to get right, so we will look at the role of communications in that later. But first, let's take a look at how deals are so well-placed to leverage the power of the story.

The rise and fail of the corporate storyteller

First off, it's important to distinguish here between the storytelling skills a dealmaking CEO needs and what has become a growing trend, and indeed what some may call an obsession, with storytelling in the wider corporate context. In fact, whole books have been written on the role of narrative and story in everything from corporate strategy to financial reporting. These should be taken with a pinch of salt.

As any real writer will tell you, one of the key things about a story is that something has to go really badly wrong (or at the very least we have to believe that it could). The audience need to feel that their protagonist and hero is in some way lost, with absolutely no hope, before the final act when resolution can come, though still at some price and with some long-term impact in terms of self-realization and change.

Now, it's easy to see that model is not quite what the chief financial officer (CFO) will have in mind when they brief an agency to create some narrative around their annual results. What they really mean is something else: making some sort of connection, usually through establishing a causal relationship, between financial figures and events that might otherwise seem unconnected or arbitrary. So, instead of the CFO saying that the company spent an extra £50 million on staff, £20 million on opening a new warehouse and doubled the R&D budget, they say, 'We invested in R&D to develop new products, trained our people in using them and increased our warehouse space to cope with the higher volumes that resulted'.

Those events have been linked by cause and effect and it's a much better way to communicate, but it's clearly a long way from passing what we might call the 'Hollywood' story test. But deals are the big exception, because they *are* one of the few areas of corporate life that really live up to the hype and deserve the story treatment.

> ### WHY DEALS PASS THE STORY TEST
>
> - High stakes – not just in terms of money, but also the future of the company and its employees.
> - We care – witness the Kraft/Cadbury deal from Chapter 5 when national interest, childhood chocolate bar memories and even whole communities were in play.
> - Jeopardy – the hero's head is (figuratively speaking) on the block because it's not unusual for CEOs to resign or be forced out after botched takeovers (the acquirer) or successful ones (the acquired).
> - Intrigue – stories need twists and turns – and deals provide plenty, with rebuttals, counteroffers, mudslinging and uncertainty – and of course 'the deal ain't done til it's done'.
> - Clear outcomes – the deal either goes through or it doesn't, there's no middle ground.
> - And a 'happy ever after' – despite all the above, these stories don't end at the end. We need to feel that the key player(s) will live on and prosper, preferably changed for the better (and a big tick for M&A deals on that score).

Why does all that matter? Because stories are one of the most powerful human forces of all. There are many theories about why that may be, going back far into history, but the simple fact is that our brains are hard wired to appreciate, understand and be persuaded by stories.

Not only do deals pass the story test with honours, they have a heap of added pressures piled on top. A Hollywood scriptwriter often imagines a world, then populates it with characters over which they have complete control. In a deal, not only are there myriad voices or stakeholders with something to say on the matter, but each will have a different take on the narrative and – thanks to technology in general and social media in particular – their own platform to say it.

Before we look at those pressures in more detail, how they differ according to stakeholder and how today's deal environment and indeed technology is intensifying those pressures, let's take a quick lesson from the archives.

> **RIGHT IDEA, WRONG MESSAGE: THE PRU AND HOW NOT TO DO IT**
>
> The value of looking at examples of deals from previous decades is that with 20/20 hindsight, the wrongs and rights are often so much clearer than today. We'll explain why that may be a bit later, but for now it's 2010 and Tidjane Thiam is CEO of the Prudential, a UK-listed, FTSE 100 insurer with growing global interests. Having weathered the global financial crisis of 2007–2008 in comparatively good shape, the Prudential were keen to get their hands on the 'jewel in the crown' of emerging market insurers, AIA, the Asian arm of cash-strapped US insurance company AIG (Reuters, 2010).
>
> The logic of the deal was there for all to see – access to high-quality assets in a fast-growing insurance market with huge future potential. Yes, the £24 billon size of the deal was challenging, almost on a par with the Prudential's market cap at the time of around £28 billion, and it was announced at a time when investor confidence was still recovering after the financial crisis. But otherwise, it looked like a sound deal.
>
> Yet within weeks it had all collapsed, attracting the ire of not only investors but regulators. And its failure came down to one word: communication. Or rather the lack of it.

> The Prudential had failed to explain this huge strategic shift, meaning that investors and shareholders were alienated rather than engaged. A failure to communicate with the Financial Services Authority not only delayed the rights issue designed to raise capital for the deal, it also led to the Prudential receiving a £30 million fine, at the time one of the largest ever imposed in the UK. And crucially, the company also committed the cardinal storytelling sin of forgetting their audience. While busily wooing new investors in Asia, they neglected their existing shareholders, whose votes could and indeed did kill the deal stone dead.

The important note here is that the deal rationale was not the problem. Four years later, Tidjane Thiam told investors they had missed a 'once in a lifetime opportunity' and he was almost certainly right (Gray, 2014). But by failing to sell that story to investors, regulators, employees and everyone else with a financial and emotional stake in the deal, he'd written his own ending. And it wasn't a happy one.

Research carried out around the time of Prudential's proposed deal showed that a fairly simple solution was actually at hand – hiring PR specialists with a track record in deal communications. Back then, the Mergers and Acquisitions Research Centre at Bayes Business School at City, University of London looked at nearly 200 deals taking place before 2010 (Faelten et al, 2014). It found that deals with PR firms on board had a significantly higher chance of completion. Only 68 per cent of deals completed successfully without PR advisers, while 91 per cent got to the finishing line when both the buyer and target company had PR advisers on their teams.

Can you hear me? Why communication is getting tougher

If the Prudential's problems were largely self-inflicted, we're now in a world where, increasingly, even those doing all the right things in terms of communication are still liable to be blown off course by forces beyond their control.

So, as in other chapters, we're going to take a brief look at how the current deal environment and changing nature of deals is impacting this aspect of the deal process. After that, we'll take a look at how technology is shifting the dial, then hear from those on the sharp end, interviewing key figures at a leading PR and reputation management company.

> COMMUNICATION – THE BASICS IN A BOX
>
> The role of communications within the deal process is wide ranging – it not only runs through every stage of the deal process but also requires engagement with, and messaging for, each stakeholder.
>
> FIGURE 6.1 The role of communication during the deal process
>
>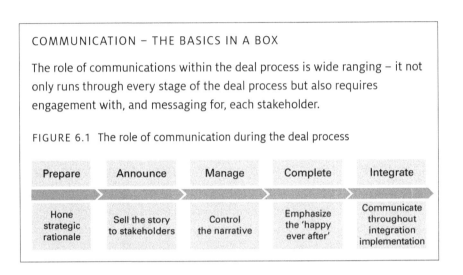

The key drivers that make communication more challenging

Many of these factors will be familiar from other chapters. Throughout the book, we've talked about the factors reshaping deals, from the need for acquirers to move out of their comfort zone to the push to carry out more deals at greater speeds.

Here, the impact on communication is clear. The fact that companies are now increasingly likely to acquire outside of their industry sector or geographic market is likely to present greater communication challenges simply because your current investors and employees may need to take more of a mental leap to see the benefits of acquiring a company from a different area than if you were, to use a sports analogy, playing at home. Similarly, strong competition for hot targets, particularly those with tech capabilities, means acquirers have to act fast, putting greater pressure on communication teams if they are to stay ahead of developments.

There are, however, three areas where changes in dealmaking and the deal environment are presenting more complex communication challenges. These are all worthy of greater investigation, particularly as they all relate to technology.

In the technology age, communicating with people matters more

Using a broad brush stroke to paint a picture of deal trends, we can identify two different types of deal. The first is a more traditional one, which involves a company buying a rival in order to boost market share and create cost synergies by eliminating areas of duplication such as production and sales channels. The second, and increasingly common type of deal, involves a larger company buying a smaller one, sometimes in a different sector, in order to get the capabilities that will help the buyer remain relevant in a rapidly changing business world.

Now, it doesn't take a genius to work out that those vital capabilities in the second deal category will be far less effective if the people who actually design, manage and maintain those capabilities aren't still on board, post-deal.

So, while the traditional deal model often involves making people redundant because their positions and capabilities were surplus to requirements in the new parent organization, the second deal category just mentioned, often motivated by the need to build technology capabilities, is more about retention. Here, it's a paradox that the growing importance of technology is actually making the people more central, increasing the need to retain them during and after an acquisition. In terms of the impact on communications, the PR messaging has gone from being all about managing the bad news that a significant chunk of employees may lose their jobs to motivating people to stick around for the so-called 'happy ever after'. In other words, it's gone from redundancy to retention, and from staff worrying about hanging onto their jobs to the acquirer worrying about hanging onto the staff.

And those acquirers have every reason to be worried. A study by J. Daniel Kim found that over one-third of acquired workers leave in the first year after their company is acquired (Kim, 2020). Although the study focused on the technology start-up world, and as a result is not representative of wider business, it is very much relevant given the trend towards companies acquiring technology capabilities, which is making even the biggest players do their 'shopping' in the world of early-stage companies. So, with the prospect of losing a third of your prized talent within a year, there is a very strong incentive to communicate clearly and effectively with those employees before, during and after the deal. We'll discuss how that's done, aided or obstructed by technology, later.

More stakeholders matter more

A dealmaker and their PR team would probably split the communications challenge in two.

The first stage is about building support prior to the announcement of the deal. That involves communicating with your own institutional investors and also, ideally, those of the target company. It's about getting your message in front of them ahead of anyone else, ensuring that the news of the deal doesn't come as a surprise and just as importantly selling the story in terms of why the deal will be a good strategic fit. Reputation is also key here because, no matter how good the story, if the key players aren't trusted, then the audience is unlikely to go along with it. So, a lot of this stage is about careful preparation, from shoring up reputation to carefully honing messaging and plans.

The second stage, post-announcement (or leak), is much harder to control because the deal is now public knowledge. Investors may still be the primary audience, including activist shareholders (those who want the company to take a specific action to improve performance) but there are also plenty of other players to consider, all of which will have their own take on the bid as well as the power to damage or even derail it.

Whether it's the rise of so-called stakeholder capitalism, which means a company must now satisfy the needs of everyone from its employees and customers to society and the planet, or simply because of greater levels of public awareness, the simple fact is that dealmakers must prepare for challenges from more sources. From energy and technology security to carbon footprint and diversity, the deal will likely be examined from every angle and anyone or indeed everyone may have an opinion – as well as a platform to air it.

Technology platforms drive change

That brings us nicely onto the final and by far the most important change in deal communication – the rise in what we could call social media channels or, more broadly, self-publishing or unfiltered communications. In one way, this is nothing new, Facebook launched in 2004, Twitter in 2006, and both were preceded by the likes of GeoCities, Friendster, MySpace and Second Life, plus all manner of online message boards and chat rooms. The real difference today, perhaps, is the way those channels are being wielded and by whom. Early Twitter was seemingly the website of choice for pop stars or bored teenagers but by 2018 the President of the United States was using it to set foreign policy, victims of workplace harassment were using it to bring down media empires and in 2022, Elon Musk was using Twitter to announce that he was buying Twitter itself (Massie, 2022).

It's also a very public form of debate, which might sound like no problem for the experienced communicator but when you think about traditional deal comms, they tend to be tightly controlled, almost entirely one-way and all emanating from the CEO and board. What happens when the bit-part player, whether that be a disgruntled employee or an investor with an agenda, now has access to the same megaphone? Worse still, what if a country's Takeover Code regulations mean your comms team can only make announcements at certain times depending on when public markets are open, but your dissenting voices can do what they want whenever they want and wherever they want.

That ongoing tension between the need to control the narrative and the difficulty of doing so in our technology-driven, multichannel 24/7/365 world is the biggest challenge. It also has a clear mirror in storytelling, where the traditional Hollywood narrative is now coming under fire from audiences who increasingly expect greater interaction and power over outcomes. They don't just want to be sold a story, they want to be part of the action.

So, let's hear what our industry experts have to say before returning to this subject and looking a little deeper into whether dynamic entrepreneurs like Elon Musk are ripping up the rule book on deal comms or demonstrating why it needs to stay the same.

Clear and simple: how the professionals do it

Headland is a London-based reputation and communications consultancy, led by founder CEO Chris Salt, with a strong track record in helping companies, including at every stage of M&A. Lucy Legh and Stephen Malthouse are partners at Headland, where they co-lead the capital markets and financial communications team.

They believe that the first key to successful deal communication is starting early: 'If you're doing it from a standing start, no matter how effective your story or which channel or technology you use, you're going to have a much harder task,' explains Lucy.

The good news here is that the value of communication professionals in M&A is now much better recognized. Chris Salt provides a telling overview on the subject: 'At one time you'd be appointed last on the list of professional advisers. Now we are often the first appointment.' They all agree that one driver for this is the recognition that reputation is key, throughout the deal process and specifically in determining valuation as well as aiding the recruitment retention that is now so vital during M&A.

They have some intriguing insights into what makes a successful deal. Given our focus earlier in the chapter on story, and this book's interest in the people and technology aspects of dealmaking, it's interesting that they highlight a human element or 'secret sauce'.

Lucy explains how the likes of PE houses spend a lot of time raking over the numbers but there has to be something else, 'Otherwise it doesn't go through. There's got to be a compelling rationale. It isn't just about the maths. It's how you tell the story.' So, it has to make sense on paper, but it also needs to connect with those individuals striking the deal and then beyond to the investors and other stakeholders. At the risk of veering into anthropology, this mirrors one of the theories about why storytelling evolved throughout history. It was a way that large groups of humans, too numerous to all sit round the same campfire, could pass on a sense of shared purpose, belief and values.

If it's important for the story (or deal rationale, here) to be convincing, it's also vital to consider that the source is believable and reliable. So, reputation management is also a crucial part of the communications skill set. Lucy sees this within the context of the need to be aware of, and manage, a wider group of interested parties. 'Deal progress is now dictated by a broader group of stakeholders and reputation is key to winning their trust,' she says, adding that reputation is also increasingly important in the valuation of a company.

Throughout this book, we have described the pressure on companies to do deals, not just to grow in size by taking out competitors but also to acquire the capabilities to stay relevant in rapidly changing markets. 'Every company is always thinking about a deal,' continues Lucy, which makes it clear how important it is not only to have the right target and message in place, but also to constantly maintain the reputations of the companies involved in the deal.

The role of technology: extending reach

Lucy and Stephen are in little doubt that technology is changing the game in deal communications.

First, in terms of reach. The use of, for example, video conferencing rather than face-to-face meetings means that more ground can be covered, more quickly. 'The management team can have one-to-one or group meetings with a wider array of shareholders at very short notice,' says Stephen. Both agree that getting people together remains vital, whether virtually or in person. 'When you get the management team in front of shareholders, things start to change; you can start to persuade people with the right story,' he continues. Stephen describes the impact as 'a synergy between human touch, storytelling and technology'. Note how these factors work together here, without friction and not in opposition.

The ability of technology to expand reach is also about the channels available in today's deal market, from professional networking tools like LinkedIn to social media channels including Twitter. There's the potential for bidders to leverage existing networks and followers' targets in the interests of the deal and set up new channels such as dedicated websites or social media accounts in advance so that they are ready to go once the deal goes live.

The role of technology: adding insight

As well as increasing reach, Lucy and Stephen believe technology can also yield greater insight, 'firstly, in terms of really understanding where the sentiment is,' as Stephen puts it.

We heard from our data analysts in Chapter 5 about how social media can be mined and ranked in terms of positive and negative sentiment during due diligence. This is clearly an area where reputation, communications and PR agencies can apply technology to measure, rate and monitor a company's standing and public perceptions about their proposed deal. There's also the possibility of beta-testing different messages to assess their effectiveness before release, and then using software to monitor any resulting shift in sentiment.

It also provides an opportunity to continuously monitor what interested parties, key commentators and other influencers are saying and therefore gain insight into how best they might be sold the story or even if the story needs changing.

The role of technology: challenges

The sheer number and relentless appetite of social media platforms also offers challenges. First, their very nature: 'Everything is instant now. You're shopping in the supermarket, and a story gets broken,' explains Stephen. That 24-hour-a-day, every day of the year thirst for technology-driven content also presents more fundamental problems for deal communications. 'M&A is a highly regulated area of communications, so we have to be really careful about the rules,' says Lucy.

Currently, those rules set clear limits on communications although, as we'll explore later, some believe that they may be relaxed in future. The UK Takeover Code, for example, currently has 22 pages governing the secrecy of information related to a deal and the timing and contents of all announcements by the two companies that are merging. Indeed, the regulator currently has this issue of communication as the second of its 38 rules, which illustrates its importance. There are restrictions in that code, for example, on when a company can announce market-sensitive information, and the same is true in most other countries. So, if a story appears in social media on, for example, a Friday evening then it may not be possible for a company to address it immediately. This presented problems even in the days when Saturday or Sunday newspapers were key channels used to influence investors and the wider public. But with myriad digital channels operating constantly and largely without the same regulatory restrictions imposed on more official communications, this presents something of an existential threat for deal communicators, whose key job is to control a single, simple narrative around a deal. A tough job when multiple voices are speaking across so many channels.

While this may be less of a problem prior to deal announcement (although the ease with which news can be shared on social media is likely to increase the risk of someone leaking the deal to the press), it's in the post-announcement phase of a deal when the risk of losing control of the story is higher.

Those multiple voices also extend to stakeholders. Employees, retail investors, activist investors and consumers may all have an opinion on a particular deal and make it heard through social media, with potentially damaging impacts on everything from reputation to regulatory attention.

On the one hand, deal communicators want people to talk about the deal but they also want to be able to control the narrative. There can be little doubt technology has made that harder. For Stephen and Lucy, it still comes down to the basics of a good, simple story, supported by strong facts and delivered engagingly. If you will excuse the reference to what is still commonly recognized as one of the greatest stories ever told, they are backing the David of deal rationale against the Goliath of social media. They may well be right, not just because David was the winner, but because of the ability of a well-crafted story to cut through and capture attention.

After the deal: let's talk

So, let's move on to look at post-deal integration. We cover this subject in detail in the next chapter, *After the deal*, but the communications role is worth mentioning separately here. As explained earlier in this chapter, people are more important than ever post-deal as their skills will be vital to the new entity's future success. Here, while technology undoubtedly provides platforms for dissenting views during and after the deal, it also offers new opportunities to promote unity. As just one example, Lucy describes how Headland has helped CEOs to send personalized text messages to all employees immediately after the deal has been finalized.

More ambitious 'interaction technologies' have great potential during the integration process, helping to get more people together and continue pushing the 'deal narrative', for example celebrating integration milestones and joint wins, updating employees on key decisions, taking questions in chat rooms and, of course, holding virtual versions of the traditional 'town hall' meetings.

While many of these technology-enabled possibilities produce greater opportunities to interact and thereby reduce employee uncertainty and increase retention, there is a caveat. These channels will be viewed as 'official', making it likely that any employees who feel disappointed by the deal or the impact of the integration process may be very careful about how they express their dissatisfaction and to whom. So, as is so often the case, no matter how smart the comms strategy or high-tech the channel by which it is delivered, it may come back to people, or should that be 'person', to fix the problem. Someone who can sell the deal internally and externally but is sensitive to what key employees may be thinking, even if they're not saying it out loud or virtually. Ring any bells? It takes us back to the opening of the chapter and the importance of a CEO who is a good storyteller. It also highlights the need for authenticity. While acknowledging that 'authentic' is at risk of becoming a vastly overused adjective, often to describe people who don't measure up to the epithet, it is key here. That's because it's not just what you say or how you say it, it's who says it. Are they credible? A communicator understands that but a computer may not.

Stephen also sees scope for technology to add value earlier in the deal process, when all the key participants, from lawyers and finance professionals to senior management, first get together. Here, he believes, each party brings their own perspective but 'we're only really scratching the surface' in terms of insight into the full rationale and benefits of the deal. He believes that this sort of technology is in the early stages, 'but I'll be really surprised if, in the near to medium term, there aren't some big innovations', he says. Watch this space.

Summing up: comms technology makes people stand out

So far, we have heard how technology is playing an important role in deal communications, from making it easier to reach key investors and other stakeholders to analysing data to uncover greater insight. Both areas should see greater scope in the future, as video technology and data visualization tools make it easier to communicate and 'deepen' the message, while the ability to 'read' sentiment across structured and unstructured data makes it easier for communicators to test messages and monitor their impact.

We have also seen how people remain crucial to the process. Communicators need to make sure that fact and argument are accompanied by the other 'signals' that we humans need. That means wrapping up the rationale in a convincing story and also ensuring that the storyteller is a person who is trusted and perceived to really mean what they're saying. If that seems a bit fluffy for the hard-edged and fast-moving world of dealmaking then just consider how the word 'authenticity' has gone from a new-age buzzword to the heart of commercial discussions around everything from business leadership to consumer buying decisions. Whether you are an investor weighing up the odds or an employee thinking about jumping ship, it's the authenticity of the message that matters here too. And that authenticity is always likely to have a human form.

But there's a danger that all of this is either scribbling in the margins or adopting broad generalities when stood up alongside the big challenge facing deal communications. Just at the time when it's already harder and harder to control the narrative because everyone has their own voice and loudhailer, the whole deal communications world may be in danger of disruption.

We talked about Elon Musk's dramatic and well-publicized bid for Twitter in Chapter 5 in the context of due diligence, but it's also highly relevant in terms of deal communications. In that context, it was initially framed as something of a disaster – a 'how not to' in making a deal announcement without thinking through the consequences. Yet despite 'jumping the gun' with a seemingly spur-of-the-moment bid announcement, he was able to see the deal through to completion.

Despite the many commentators who criticized his instinctive approach, it did have some advantages in the early stages of the bid. Like many great battlefield moves, it puts the target under fire immediately with no time to prepare. It is also a great example of authenticity. Not only did the news of the bid come from Musk's own Twitter account, it also clearly embodied everything that he's about – decisive, wealthy, tech-obsessed and disruptive.

In terms of communication, it's interesting that Musk also chose to engage with Twitter employees during the bid rather than waiting until completion. In addition, he did so directly. At the 16 June 2022 Q&A session with Twitter, Musk was reported to have said, 'Some people use their hair to express themselves; I use Twitter. I find it's the best forum for communicating with a lot of people simultaneously, and getting that message directly to people' (Ghaffary, 2022). Those who opt to follow Musk's approach to communication in the future may find life easier in that respect as some commentators believe that technology may force regulators to relax the current rules on communication during public deals.

The final paradox here is that a technology platform seems to favour human authenticity more highly than the traditional, people-run forms of communication it is replacing. That may prove to be consequential. While deal communications professionals can expertly finesse messaging throughout the deal, they are tied by regulation and, perhaps partly as result, to certain ways of operating which can be centralized and slow to respond. On the other hand, there are signs that regulation governing deal communications may be relaxed, allowing a more even playing field. It's also worth noting that any deal runs the risk of a higher profile activist investor, such as we saw above with Elon Musk, entering the fray. So, the vast majority of deal participants will still benefit from professional comms advisers – and any who face a social media-savvy opponent like Musk are likely to need more help than ever.

> KEY POINTS
>
> - Technology is improving communication at every stage of the deal process, from measuring employee/investor sentiment to distributing messages more effectively.
> - But human judgement and authenticity will always be key to getting those messages right and selling the story to investors and other stakeholders.
> - While the proliferation of platforms makes it harder for communicators to control the narrative from deal announcement to completion, interactive technology can improve post-deal communication. This can support integration and deliver better deal outcomes.
> - With deal communication currently strictly regulated, the scene is set for disruption by entrepreneurs who can leverage the power of social media. However, professional reputation and communications support will likely remain vital and the human appetite for story will endure.

References

Faelten, A, Singh, J, Moeller, S and Badham, D (2014), Selling the Story, M&A Research Centre, Bayes Business School, December, www.finyear.com/attachment/551635/ (archived at https://perma.cc/KX3Q-ELJN)

Ghaffary, S (2022) What you need to know about Elon Musk's big meeting with Twitter employees, *Vox*, 16 June, www.vox.com/recode/23171474/elon-musk-twitter-meeting (archived at https://perma.cc/8TX2-3WJQ)

Gray, A (2014) Pru chief laments missed AIA opportunity, *Financial Times*, 12 August, www.ft.com/content/c0a9de12-21fc-11e4-9d4a-00144feabdc0 (archived at https://perma.cc/QTU4-4MH4)

Kim, J D (2020) Startup acquisitions as a hiring strategy: worker choice and turnover, 1 March, https://papers.ssrn.com/sol3/papers.cfm?abstract_id=3252784 (archived at https://perma.cc/6NH8-AFFS)

Massie, G (2022) Elon Musk sends first tweet after buying Twitter, *The Independent*, 25 April, www.independent.co.uk/tech/elon-musk-twitter-tweet-today-b2065220.html (archived at https://perma.cc/77EA-5LZT)

Nadella, S (2016) Satya Nadella email to employees on acquisition of LinkedIn, *Microsoft News Center*, 13 June, https://news.microsoft.com/2016/06/13/satya-nadella-email-to-employees-on-acquisition-of-linkedin/ (archived at https://perma.cc/94RN-2KBM)

Reuters Staff (2010) Britain's Prudential in talks to buy AIA: report, *Reuters*, 27 February, www.reuters.com/article/us-prudential-aia-idUS-TRE61Q1DJ20100227 (archived at https://perma.cc/4GMD-PBXV)

7

After the deal

Why integration is the most critical and people-sensitive stage of the deal cycle and how technology is helping to support more successful outcomes

This chapter focuses on the last stage of the deal process but it's by no means the least important one, as post-merger integration is where all the hard-won benefits of the deal are realized – or not. No matter how smart the deal strategy and target identification, how keen the deal price and how thorough the due diligence, if the two companies fail to integrate successfully and thereby don't achieve the identified synergies that drove the deal in the first place, then it will all be for nothing.

Remember those dispiriting figures from Bayes Business School in London earlier in the book, showing that less than 50 per cent of all deals are successful? Those unfortunate metrics are based entirely on what happens *after* the deal. While paying too high a price or failing to do proper due diligence will invariably have some impact on post-deal performance, by far the biggest factor will be how the new entity capitalizes on its newly combined resources, position in the market, and additional capabilities, products or services. One can work hard to recover from paying too high a price or realizing too late that there may have been a better target company, but it is almost impossible to turn around a failed integration.

Yet, paradoxically, integration is probably the area of the deal cycle that gets the least attention. Perhaps because, although it's absolutely crucial to the outcome of the deal, integration is rarely central to the mechanics of getting the deal done, falling far behind more pressing negotiations and contractual arrangements. Even though all parties will understand that integration is both a key driver of the deal and crucial to its ultimate success, our authors have found through experience that most key players are not fully engaged with it prior to deal closure and tend to think of it as 'less sexy and headline-grabbing' and 'something that will just happen'. We're getting our first hint here of how human factors – for example our tendency to prioritize short-term imperatives over long-term benefits or being wary of joining another 'tribe' during the integration process – are crucial at this stage of the deal process. So, although, as we'll explain in due course, technology has a large and growing role to play in integration, its success often depends on support from essential human abilities, particularly communication.

Not so fast: the complications of integration

We humans like to keep it simple. While the fictional and famously logical Mr Spock from *Star Trek* would have no problem getting his mind around deal price and any twists and turns before the deal is struck, once that's over even he may struggle.

There may be talk, pre-deal, about potential synergies, typically naming a number that will be achieved by, for example, reducing headcount, simplifying distribution channels, combining product lines and closing a plant here or there. All that sounds admirably simple and logical, but after the deal, it inevitably gets more complex, no matter how difficult you thought it would be when it was planned out. It may be harder than previously thought to achieve those much-sought-after efficiency gains or, even if attained, those cost savings or revenue benefits may be outweighed by unforeseen upfront costs, investments, or poor planning and communication when integrating the two companies.

> **PAINTING A MURKY PICTURE: THE UNCLEAR ROUTE TO INTEGRATION**
>
> Let's suppose that our fictional paint manufacturer from Chapter 3, having taken over its closest local rival, no longer needs to maintain two sales and distribution teams. Perhaps it can go further still – by making all the new entity's paints in one factory rather than two, reducing its combined product range slightly and maybe even eliminating one size of paint can. After all, how many shades of off-white can anyone really need? The result would be significant cost savings achieved through sensible, logical synergies.
>
> But what if, after forcing through all these cost and revenue synergies, they find out too late that their former rivals' customers had enjoyed a highly personalized relationship with the original sales team and resent the 'one sizing' of their paint manufacturer's product range. As an unforeseen consequence, having laid off the acquired company's sales force, most of whom have now joined a rival, huge numbers of customers may have been lost forever. And the customers who previously bought cans of *Pale Sand* can't find it anymore and insist that *Sandy White* just isn't the same shade, despite all the marketing efforts that prove that it is. That seemingly well-priced, strategy-led deal is starting to not look so clever anymore. Note here the link between integration and strategy. And also see the connection with due diligence – if the acquiring paint company had looked more closely at its target's customer base before signing the deal, it might have paid less (note the connection with price) or formulated a different integration strategy.

Two sides of the coin: integration winners and losers

So much for fictional examples; let's look at two real historic post-deal integrations.

In 2005, US telecommunication provider Sprint acquired a majority stake in its rival Nextel in a landmark $37.8 billion deal (United States Securities and Exchange Commission, 2006), making the combined entity number three in the US market, with only AT&T and Verizon sitting above them (Woodsworth and Penniman, 2013). The logic seemed powerful in a sector where consolidation offered opportunities to cut costs as well as build brands and grow. But the reality proved entirely different, with technologies and corporate cultures proving incompatible, driven by Sprint's place in the traditional consumer market and Nextel's more innovative and entrepreneurial origins serving business customers. What looked to be complementary businesses turned out to be very different to each other. Seeing few career prospects ahead as Sprint dominated senior executive positions in the combined entity, many of Nextel's brightest and best left. By early 2008, $30 billion of the deal had been written down.

The second example is from the other side of the ocean. In 2009, Centrica, the UK's biggest utility provider, completed a hostile takeover of Venture Productions, a nimble and highly innovative oil and gas exploration company (Milner, 2009). But remember we said that integration was inherently complex? Well, this time it worked out. This was largely because Centrica acquired Ventura to use the acquisition to change their own corporate culture, instil nimbleness and agility and introduce innovation. Therefore, Centrica made concerted efforts to keep key Venture people onboard, motivated, and with an opportunity to not only retain authority within their own business but to also benefit from the broader opportunities and resources offered by the merged group. The integration teams had focused early on the culture, people and communication issues and ensured they were addressed head-on and therefore would not interfere with the integration.

Be careful about making assumptions

It's important to be aware that, despite both examples being technology-focused companies, there is little mention of technology when it comes to integration. That's primarily because, as the least analysis- and data-driven and the most people- and culture-dependent of the deal process, the technologies of the early 2000s were seen to have little application. Where it does get a mention it's in the context of the integration of the IT systems, infrastructure and applications of the two companies.

Times have changed and computers are now able to take on much more 'human' tasks. In fact, if this book has taught us one thing so far, it is to be very cautious about any assumption that there are certain things that only humans can do. From playing poker to deal negotiation, it rarely turns out to be clear cut. So, despite the traditional view that integration is all about human factors, technology can play an important role in making it more successful, if applied correctly and at the right time.

Adding grist to the mill: the barriers to integration

Before we look at the role of technology in helping dealmakers with the integration process, it's important to identify the barriers.

Let's begin with the simple truth that the earlier stages of the deal cycle are, well, just simpler. Facts, money and legal niceties rule as price and terms are agreed. Even the people element can be relatively straightforward, and not only because the number of people is smaller, with perhaps only the two CEOs working out the 'heads of agreement' and ultimately shaking hands to do the deal. Yes, it's important for the CEO and acquirer to feel they can work with each other but the nitty gritty of how that will happen is usually left for later. As an aside, it's worth noting that at each stage of the deal, more people get involved as the deal teams get larger and ultimately – in the final integration phase – every employee needs to be engaged in making it successful.

In any deal, that 'left for later' in-box pile is likely to be full, and it is only likely to get more so once the transaction has been completed. This is a critical point often overlooked: in the pressured dealmaking world where everyone is driving toward the high-profile and exciting announcement and consummation of the deal, the softer and more difficult (often employee- and customer-related) issues get added to a list of 'to do's' once there's time to address them in integration. The same goes for technology integration, which is often recognized as being important but also complex. That means there is a lot to do after the deal is signed, and often these are the areas where differences can't be reconciled, such as the unquantifiable areas like cultural differences between the two organizations or the unknown reactions of customers. Clearly, any technology that could lessen the in-tray pile would be welcome.

There are also structural aspects of the deal process that mitigate against successful integration. We have alluded to it in several of the chapters so far, but one key factor revolves around the unwillingness of either or both parties to reveal more information than is absolutely necessary before the deal is closed. This impacts integration because making any realistic appraisal of how well the two companies might work together in the future may require far more information than either side would usually be comfortable with revealing until the deal is signed. Both sides want to look as attractive to each other as possible, while also avoiding revealing information that could be valuable to the other or a rival in case the deal falls apart.

As we conjectured in Chapter 5, it's the absence of information that – if you will forgive our stereotyping – tends to bring out the best in the traditional, tight-lipped, square-jawed dealmaker of yore. Perhaps that's one reason why 'fluffier' but absolutely vital disciplines like HR can sometimes find it tough to get a seat at the table during the pre-closing process. Even if they are consulted it is perhaps more likely to be about the costs associated with downsizing workforces rather than how talent can be best managed, or culture best measured, to ensure successful integration. But sadly, HR is too often one of the last to join the deal table. One of the authors was told several years ago by the partner of a large human resources consultancy that approximately 40 per cent of HR directors found out about a merger or acquisition of their company from the public press release. In such a situation, it's not surprising that the strategy and deal selection process, if not much of the due diligence, ignored many of the crucial HR issues that would cause problems in the later integration phases.

More barriers: earn-outs and transitional service agreements

We'll be hearing more about this subject from our interviewees but there is another potential structural barrier to integration: the earn-out. It's common for key players in the acquired company to be tied to the new entity for a fixed period, during which time they usually have pre-arranged targets they must meet in order to maximize rewards. This makes sense because it retains and motivates key staff while also, in theory at least, helping the acquirer to achieve their performance objectives. However, it can also provide a barrier to integration, because those key staff are incentivized to hit their own targets, rather than those of the new entity as a whole. Add to that the practical difficulties for a selling founder or management shareholder of operating under an earn-out within the acquiring company. They may, for example, be under pressure to maximize profits within their individual business unit in order to reach a pre-arranged target, with no motivation or incentive to cooperate with new colleagues and drive organization-wide synergies.

That barrier has something of a mirror image at a company, contractual level. Typically, in a divestment, the selling company will agree to a TSA to guarantee, in essence, that its services and systems are kept up and running for a fixed period, post-deal. This is to ensure that buyers don't end up with a service or structure that they can't or don't know how to operate because the seller 'takes the money and runs'. While, once again, this has inescapable logic, it can also have the downside of making integration more difficult. That's because, under the TSA, not only is the seller expected to keep the service up and running, but the buyer is committed to keeping the infrastructure that supports it more or less unchanged. After all, it would hardly be fair for the buyer to guarantee certainty of service if the buyer keeps changing the processes underlying it.

While the arrangement provides welcome certainty, it can hold back progress. As a result, there is growing momentum, particularly in faster-moving sectors like tech, to not only change the duration and scope of TSAs, which can be as long as three years for central areas such as enterprise resource planning (ERP) systems, but also, as we'll explore later in the chapter, to use technology to create a better 'bridge'.

Bringing down the barriers

So, to summarize our discoveries so far, while integration is the only real measure of post-deal success, it is also inherently complex because it combines high financial stakes with unpredictable human factors, and it faces a number of structural barriers that are built into the deal process. Just as William Shakespeare has Richard III calling out in frustration, 'A horse, a horse, my kingdom for a horse', our dealmakers have never been more in need of a helping hand from technology. But how effective can it ever be in such a people-centred world?

Before we hear from the practitioners navigating these difficulties to create highly successful businesses built on well-integrated acquisitions, let's look at the current role of technology in post-deal integration.

The role of technology in addressing integration barriers

Sadly, there's no single silver bullet; it's more of a shotgun approach, with several smart technologies attacking the various enemies to integration.

The first volley comes from analytics and AI solutions that aim to identify where synergies can be achieved, as we discussed in Chapter 4. These can map both buyer and seller organizations, including their IT and broader technology capabilities, to home in on synergies.

Readers may already have spotted the potential flaw. Like any analytics tool, its performance is likely to be only as good as its data yet, until the deal is closed, access to that data may be limited to avoid giving away vital information. While identifying synergies and developing integration strategies after the deal is valuable, it's already too late to avoid overpaying for an indigestible asset by failing to see the obstacles to a happy future relationship.

But technology providers do have one answer: the clean room, which is essentially a technology-powered relation to the data room run by a 'clean team'. It is a safe space where, before closing, both sides can access data that is then processed by a third-party provider who reveals its findings. In other words, the buyer and seller do not need to (if you'll forgive the well-worn expression) 'open the kimono' to each other, just to a third party who is sworn to secrecy.

At their best, these clean rooms offer the opportunity not only to identify synergies but also to start designing the future state of the new, combined entity. That's because, in simple terms, they can plug in the systems and data from both the acquirer and buyer. A cloud-based platform can then draw insights from the combined data without any disruption to the day-to-day running of those systems.

Even the thorny problem of earn-outs and TSAs, which could restrict the initial integration of systems, promises to be at least partially addressable through technology. Without wishing to get too technical, the old solution was to either keep the buyer's system up and running or build a clone of it within the acquirer's system. The new solution is to use SaaS to move it to the acquirer 'lock, stock and barrel'. This also means that the seller does not need to maintain their existing infrastructure and the buyer can focus on other aspects of the integration process, provided the TSAs have been adjusted accordingly.

Through technologies like those described so far, acquirers are able to get a 'head start' on integration, even before the deal is signed off. That means not only getting the new entity to its desired target state faster and with less risk, but also exploring earlier and in more detail if the integration plans are both achievable and desirable.

It would be naïve to assume that there are not some limitations to these applications at present; access to data before the deal closes can still be an issue – whether due to commercial or regulatory sensitivity – and there are also some question marks around how well the integration opportunities modelled by technology will actually work in reality. But the tools are getting better and even in their present form they still have value as, at the very least, a 'sandpit' for exploring and modelling outcomes. However, as we'll discover from our experts later in this chapter, the tendency of humans to jump up and down on those sandcastles should not be underestimated.

A successful, technology-led integration

But first let's look at an example of where technology does triumph. The first point to note about this type of tool (a third-party technology platform) is that it is not purely post-deal as it offers users support throughout the deal cycle, from target identification to valuation to due diligence. As such, it can leverage the information loaded and learned from earlier stages to add greater value and also more efficiently and quickly later in the process than previously had been possible.

The 2019 combination of Fiserv, Inc and First Data, two Fintech companies specializing in online payment solutions (EY, 2022), made perfect sense on paper. Each had built dominance within their own link of the financial payment transaction chain, but together they felt that they could be stronger.

The underlying logic for the $22 billion deal (Tech Monitor, 2019) – a set of complementary capabilities and complementary clients – was compelling, but grafting together these two complex businesses with over 45,000 employees had challenges.

With the stakes so high, they turned to a third-party technology platform that used its own AI and advanced analytics tools to support integration. It was a process that involved millions of clients and billions of data points and targeted areas of duplication, the streamlining of technology infrastructure, increasing operational efficiencies, and optimizing overall organizational footprint.

It worked. Within eight months of the deal close, the synergy target was upped from $1 billion to $1.2 billion (Tech Monitor, 2019). Today, the merged Fiserv, Inc is also efficiently cross-selling capabilities to its clients through a single, seamless, globally integrated payment solution.

Technology and the human touch

What the example illustrates well is how two companies, both built on the latest tech and both operating in very similar markets, can use a technology platform to automate many of the complex but standardized tasks involved in a merger, including integration. While tools such as these do not typically directly address cultural differences between organizations, it's easy to see how they might offer some help by, for example, avoiding many of the long hours and inevitable frustrations of trying to complete such processes. We think it's also reasonable to assume that the use of an efficient, third-party technology could also help to avoid some, but certainly not all, of the inevitable conflicts that arise, post-deal, about who gets to do what and who gets what done to them. Another example, perhaps, of how technology can remove some of the tension around human interactions.

One of our interviewees for this chapter noted how one of the barriers to integration is that employees of acquired companies must, typically, immediately adjust to using their acquirer's technology systems for even the most mundane tasks. It may sound like a small point, but it's an interesting insight into how technology can impact individuals – in this case quickly stripping them of a competence that they had previously taken for granted.

There is also a tendency, when thinking of technology, to assume that we are referring to the shiniest and most intuitive of new systems. The reality is far from the truth. Often, what acquirers find are euphemistically referred to as legacy systems, which lack compatibility and thereby hinder integration. The risks of upgrading, let alone switching to a single new system are simply so great that they get kept on a form of life support, making full integration almost impossible.

Even if an acquirer is lucky enough to buy a company that has brilliant and updated technology, the problems of integration aren't over because that incredible platform almost certainly comes with a brilliant technology team. And that team may be highly resistant to changing even a single line of code in a system that is 'working fine, thank you', let alone allowing its platform to be leveraged for different uses for which it wasn't designed in the first place. So do you stand up to those technology staff and risk them leaving the company, destroying the value of your acquisitions as the door swings shut behind them? Or do you decide to put their integration on the 'leave until later' pile? Our interviewees will have an answer to that quandary later in the chapter, but it highlights a bigger point around the changing nature of deals, which we must first explore.

Different deal drivers, different integration

Traditionally, the value realized by deals centred around eliminating duplication to cut costs, increasing market share and gaining benefits of scale. The logic was that the combined revenues, minus the cost savings generated post-merger, equalled greater profit. Nothing wrong with that of course, but does it reflect current realities?

As we discussed in our introduction, more companies are doing more deals and for different reasons. For example, larger acquirers are buying smaller players (so-called roll-up or bolt-on strategies) and smaller acquirers are buying new capabilities rather than just snapping up their local rival (for example, non-tech companies are acquiring tech, rather like our fictional paint manufacturer buying an app in Chapter 5 or Goldman Sachs buying digital capabilities in Chapter 1). This type of deal logic is unlikely to match up with a traditional integration strategy. If BP are buying a green energy company, is the objective to cut costs and fully integrate it into the oil and gas business? Probably not. Is our fabled paint manufacturer buying a colour-finding app (which we invented for illustrative purpose in Chapter 5) going to then hand it over to the existing sales and marketing team to manage? Unlikely.

From win-lose to win-win: integration evolves

Instead, such deals require a different approach to integration, which is probably best summed up as a win-win strategy. Put simply, you need to find the best of both worlds for both parties, so that the management and employees in the target company stay on board and are motivated. Those who have been paying attention will note a potential impact on deal culture, as we move from deals that produce a triumphant winner and a subjugated loser to ones where everyone not only comes out of the process with a positive result, but also enjoys each step of the journey. Quite clearly, that different outcome may require different skills and personal attributes. In terms of integration, those new skills will be more about working together with the acquired company's management to implement a plan that engages and delivers for all. While that may sound wishy-washy, it's simply good business sense as retaining and motivating staff is increasingly recognized as being crucial to post-integration success. Historically, some of the most value-destructive deals of all time have been where the winner imposes a plan that involves laying off many of the acquired company's staff and disempowering their senior management. A more nuanced take on the subject of integration, culture and technology came up in our introductory chapter. A participant in a post-deal integration thought that the smooth nature of the process was in no small part due to the fact that meetings were held virtually. Their theory was that the shift away from in-person meetings to video calls was a positive for integration. The reason? By giving everyone equal screen space on the calls, the technology was more conducive to collaborative progress and less vulnerable to being hijacked by one or two powerful egos resistant to change or compromise.

The rise and rise of digital value

But the bigger picture here is how technology is increasingly not merely the utility that enables a business to keep doing what it does best but is also a source of value for any acquirer.

That means thinking more broadly about digital value; understanding and quantifying the skills, capabilities and technology of both target and acquirer, then considering how they would fit into the combined organization. A target's software or CRM platform can be a vital asset but often there is hidden value in how they can be combined.

A legacy company may look to an acquisition as a way to quickly modernize its IT system. For instance, legacy companies can acquire a business that has a modern IT or ERP system and then transition their existing systems to those of the target company.

To take that value in combining technologies a step further, data is also a key element. We're increasingly seeing how data held by one company, when combined with the data and software held by another, can result in a huge uptick in value. One simple example is data from social media which, harvested in the right way and combined with other datasets, can provide highly intelligent and valuable insight into everything from stock market predictions to consumer buyer signals.

While all these elements have become key to identifying the true value of a deal, it's notable that they all add significantly to the integration burden and size of the potential synergies.

Integration and the link with digital transformation

No one knows the precise date when the words digital and transformation became inexorably wedded together but a divorce now seems unlikely so let's run with it. As long as we don't get asked to pull anything out of the transformation toolbox, we can live with it.

The serious point here is that integration, which increasingly revolves around bringing together different technology systems, often coincides with the newly emerged entity embarking on ambitious growth plans. After all, few things in a company's life are as truly transformational as a major acquisition and all the new possibilities that it creates.

So, the argument goes, why spend a lot of time and effort patching up and marrying together two different technology systems when you could have a new all-singing, all-dancing ERP system that will also enable you to make widespread, positive changes to your organization and operating model? Changes that may also help you to take advantage of the new growth opportunities ahead?

While the aspiration is good, the risks involved in combining the already tough task of integration with implementing a completely new IT infrastructure can be high, as we'll hear soon from an expert who knows all about the perils and pitfalls in this area.

Testing our case

Having laid out in this chapter the pros and pitfalls of integration, plus the important role of technology and people within it, now is the time to test it against the real-life experience of those not only doing the deals but also looking to build success after the deal.

We are fortunate, then, to have the insight of two senior executives involved in the growth, largely through acquisition, of financial news and data provider, Acuris.

Carrie Anne Holt was head of Corporate Development at Acuris until 2020, having taken the position shortly after the company, then known as Mergermarket, was acquired by private equity firm BC Partners in 2013 for £382 million. During her time at Acuris, Carrie Anne worked on the execution and integration of nine acquisitions, before BC Partners sold the majority of their stake in Acuris to financial software and data business ION Group in a £1.35 billion deal.

As chief technology officer at both Mergermarket and Acuris, Ross Heritage worked closely with Carrie Anne on many of the acquisitions and can provide a valuable perspective into the technology-related aspects of integrations.

Not all integrations are equal but some are more equal than others

Carrie Anne and Ross both make an important distinction between two types of Acuris acquisitions. Content-driven companies, which typically provide proprietary data and intelligence to subscribers, were integrated more quickly and relatively easily because:

- The rationale was clear and urgent: Acuris wanted its broader subscriber base to benefit from the new content.
- The technology requirements of integrating the new data provider were relatively simple: more a case of redirecting the pipe rather than reconfiguring the plumbing.
- The culture aspect was straightforward: the key people who came with the acquisition cared deeply about the value and veracity of their content, so welcomed the broader distribution, which carried no dilution or other potential threat to their cherished data.

The second type of acquisitions involved technology platforms. These had been built to deliver proprietary, third-party or publicly available data. In other words, they were not primarily about the data itself but about providing easy and intelligent access to it through technology. Connecting these acquired platforms together within one information architecture or single platform was often extremely challenging in terms of technology but, interestingly, both Carrie Anne and Ross described the integration journey primarily in relation to people.

That's because, for the people at the platform companies that Acuris acquired, sharing or changing technologies was the aspect they most cared about. 'They will have literally spent day and night for the best part of a decade sweating over producing their platform,' explains Ross. When it came to the coding and design of their platform, which they felt passionate about, relinquishing control was likely to be an issue. As Carrie Anne describes it, 'entrepreneurial people often don't like losing control and they can see integration as losing control'. Given that Acuris were understandably keen to retain the technology talent that had built these platforms, they trod very carefully rather than enforce integration from the beginning.

Their 'hands-off' stance was helped by the fact that, when the acquisitions began, Mergermarket simply did not have the infrastructure to integrate. 'We only started to look at integration opportunities much later,' explains Carrie Anne. Ross adds that a later, larger acquisition with a good technology platform was the accelerator for greater integration, because that platform could be leveraged more widely throughout the whole organization (see our earlier section on identifying digital value).

But it's clear that, even with such greater capabilities, it's not just a case of 'plug and play', as the needs of the new acquisition's people still have to be carefully managed. 'If we had acquired a large technical team that was used to doing things in a certain way, we had to make sure we didn't disrupt them and risk losing some of the talent,' explains Carrie Anne. Ross adds that 'it can be great technology, but unless you're actually buying the people that go with it, then everything falls flat.'

Strategy and integration at play

So, from Carrie Anne and Ross's experience, it's clear that people always come first, even in a technology-focused company. But there is another dimension. Business people are nothing if not pragmatists, so the integration process must ultimately be driven by commercial needs and not theories about how to handle people and/or technology. Carrie Anne puts it simply: 'It comes down to what your strategy is; your rationale for the acquisition in the first place.' For example, in Acuris' case they did not want a customer having to access their information via numerous Acuris channels or platforms. The need to integrate was therefore primarily driven by reducing multiple sign-ins to improve customer experience. If an acquired company got in the way of that particular objective, they had to act, even if it was likely to create ripples behind the scenes.

Ross also has an answer to our earlier question about the risk that earn-outs impede integration: it's all about selling the benefits of integration on an individual rather than company-wide level. 'If they see the upside, something that's going to help them achieve their earn-out target, then everyone's happy. If they don't, then you have to wait,' he explains.

For someone who has been at the heart of digital transformations throughout his career Ross, perhaps surprisingly, sees technology as a secondary factor. 'It will have an influence on price and it will have an influence on what happens after the deal but it is very rarely the driver', he explains. Perhaps, in part, this is because his experience in transforming companies using technology gives him the confidence that any such problems can be fixed. And he thinks that's getting easier as technology improves. 'It's now not so much about tightly integrating the tech but integrating the capabilities', he explains, citing an example of how what appears as a single app or interface to the customer can be driven by different platforms sitting behind it. It's an interesting example of how technological evolution is making 'front-end' integration easier, while keeping it simpler 'behind the wall'.

Both Carrie Anne and Ross back the idea that integration must start early and be people-centric: 'Unless you build those relationships very early on in the process, you stand very little chance of getting anything done without a whole heap of barriers,' says Carrie Anne. Ross warns that acquirers must avoid getting carried away with their own excitement about the path ahead and put themselves in the acquirers' shoes, asking, 'What is their incentive after the deal to even have a conversation about change? You're asking them to take time out of their business day and their revenue goals and their own objectives to work with you on something that's for the good of your own business.'

Words that perhaps reflect an interesting paradox. As technology has taken on more tasks and is now at the core of a company's value, people have to be even more carefully handled during integration. While the old model often focused on laying off workers after the deal, the new one appears more about keeping hold of them.

Going for gold: the people's eye view

Let's take a break from tech talk to return to something we're all experts on: human nature. So far, we've found that the real nuggets of gold are often uncovered by scraping away at assumptions about what actions only a human can do.

Our next interviewee, Adrian Moorhouse, knows all about working his way to gold, having not only topped the podium as a Great Britain Olympic swimmer but also founded successful people change and performance consultancy Lane4 Management Group.

His understanding of people and how to maximize their performance has seen him involved at the sharp end of integrations, helping big companies with large workforces to work together better after the deal. His first point is that, even when deals have the soundest commercial logic, they can still risk being derailed by people and culture conflict. One example, touched on in Chapter 5, was the post-merger integration of cost-conscious, process-driven cellular network

T Mobile and its more colourful rival Orange in 2010. Their very different cultures made the integration process harder and longer.

Culture is key and technology is helping

Adrian has thought carefully and deeply about how to really get under the hood of company culture – what it means, how it feels and, most important of all, how to fix the problems that can result from it. He's quick to point out that culture isn't always what it appears, explaining in Chapter 5 that there is 'the espoused culture, the lived culture and the deep culture'. By the latter he says he means 'something intangible that you can't really shake the roots of…'.

To you or I that might appear too hard a challenge to address, but as a gold medal-winning athlete and successful businessman, Adrian has broken it down to a simple mnemonic. As simple, in fact, as ABC: autonomy, belonging and competence. Now, as Adrian himself is quick to point out, those are an exact match with a widely known and broadly held theory around self-determination, first introduced by Deci and Ryan in their 1985 book *Self-Determination and Intrinsic Motivation in Human Behavior* (O'Hara, 2017). Here, the term self-determination refers to a person's ability to manage themselves, to make confident choices, and to think on their own.

Now if, as Adrian lays out, the root of the problems within integration is basically the same as the essential human needs laid out by Deci and Ryan, it's clear why post-deal integration can present such major problems. Essentially, it triggers deep human fears and necessities.

All those company core values, mission statements and purpose pledges that we largely took for granted are brought vividly to life during an integration if we feel that our sense of belonging is under pressure from our new partner. Autonomy is under threat as we see even our leaders playing second fiddle to the acquirer's management team. And competence is crumbling as we navigate new IT systems, managers and requirements.

Tools for change

Adrian works very closely with both sides of the deal to understand their cultures and build bridges through common objectives and mutual support: 'How do you create the "letting go" for both groups of people in a new setting where the performance environment totally changes and the culture nuances are massive?'.

Focus groups and one-to-ones are crucial ways in which Adrian identifies and addresses the obstacles to integration. But, interestingly, he also uses technology to crunch everything from survey data to interview text to scan for the cultural differences and definitions.

He also cites the work of UK-based behavioural change specialist company Tao Leadership. The firm uses analytics to better understand and change behaviours and culture. One way it does so is by identifying 'influencers' within the organization and then working with them to accelerate cultural transition.

So, even though Adrian thinks that integration is ultimately all about people, he still believes technology has a valuable role to play in helping to spot patterns and effect change.

The technologist bytes back

Our last insights are from an interviewee who appears at first glance to be from the opposite end of the spectrum to Adrian. Anthony Byrne has two decades of experience working on large technology implementations, including helping companies that have been taken over or divested by major utilities to thrive inside or outside the 'mothership'. He's also CEO of AgilityWorks, which helps companies 'realize the benefits of SAP technology'. To the layperson, that means using the latest cloud-based technology systems to create more agile and efficient ways of running organizations.

He confirms that TSAs mean that any acquisition is likely initially to be 'cut and pasted' into a larger utility rather than integrated. But he believes that's often the best option as it not only reduces risk but also reflects the reality of deal dynamics, which dictate that there is rarely much opportunity for meaningful integration planning until the deal is signed.

Getting the people in the room

Although he recognizes that there are increasingly sophisticated tools to help with the integration process pre-deal, Anthony explains that 'getting the key people in the room together is essential and that's unlikely to happen until the deal has closed. That's when you really can actually start having more productive conversations. I think before that, it's just too hard.' He also points out those key people should include IT experts. Without their early input, the risk is that individual business leaders 'start going down silos' that can impede the integration process.

That provides an interesting counterpoint to our earlier call for HR teams to have a seat at the table as early as possible in the deal process, so they can spot people and culture problems during due diligence and help smooth the path to integration. There is just as strong a case, it appears, to bring key IT players such as the chief technology officers (CTOs) to the same table. This is a point that neatly sums up the vital and complementary roles of both people and technology in the integration process. And it's one that also chimes with the more collaborative approach to integration that we discussed earlier in the chapter, driven by the changing nature of deals.

Using the window

Anthony also emphasizes the need to make the most of what he calls 'the window' that exists immediately after deal signing. 'It's not necessarily about the detail at that stage but setting out where you want to go. That is the time to talk about fuller integration and wider transformation. Set your North Star, then worry about how far and how fast you are going to follow it later.' Rather like Carrie Anne and Ross, Anthony points out that full integration is not always desirable. In his industry, tight regulation or the fact that the company has been acquired as an income-generating asset, means that in some cases the commercial logic will mitigate against integration. Spotting value is also crucial: 'Your acquired company may have a lower cost base or a better procurement system that you want to replicate across the whole organization.' Despite his two decades of experience helping companies to use technology to transform their business, he is wary about trying to integrate and transform at the same time. 'I think it's a balance, because, depending on the maturity of the leadership and the actual capability you have in the business, you may need to give away some transformation opportunities to stay safe,' he explains.

Finally, he believes that technology has potential to make integration easier, specifically the ability of cloud-based systems to identify synergies and support both parties post-deal. While he sees people as the key drivers and enablers of integration, he also sees them as the biggest obstacles – from the seller's unwillingness to 'let go' and embrace the future to the competing cultures that can get in the way.

Summing up

One of the reasons why integration is so difficult is that it requires a hard, honest look in the mirror for both the target and the acquirer, whether to truthfully appraise company culture or to be honest about any technology weaknesses. That's tough because it works against some other key elements of the deal process, which favour the need to tightly control information and reveal only that which will help you strike the best deal. But, with data and technology gradually closing the information gap between buyer and seller, there are grounds for optimism.

Other aspects of integration may also be changing for the better. The business world is becoming more aware of the impact of culture and the value of people and is therefore more likely to understand the importance of both to deal outcome success. While integration is currently often hampered by acquirers' poor technology capabilities, this will also change as the link between technology mastery and deal outcome becomes ever clearer.

Integration is – and will probably always remain – an area mostly focused on people, but those people will increasingly have to harness technology to succeed.

> KEY POINTS
>
> - Post-deal integration is often the most technically complex and people-dependent stage of the deal cycle, but it's also where true deal success lies.
> - The changing nature of deals is impacting integration, making it more and not less people-centred.
> - With technology now at the core of most companies' value, technology integration is becoming ever more important, but people are still crucial to that process.
> - Deal technology is doing more to help with integration but is often being hindered by long-standing structural barriers within the deal process.
> - People as individuals – and in terms of their collective culture – are crucial to integration and always will be. But even in this area, technology tools are already helping and have the potential to do more to address human pain points during integration.

References

EY (2022) How smart technology helped Fiserv accelerate M&A strategy, *EY*, 2022 www.ey.com/en_gl/strategy-transactions/how-smart-technology-helped-fiserv-accelerate-their-ma-strategy (archived at https://perma.cc/T5NA-PYTN)

Milner, M (2009) Centrica heads toward £1bn hostile bid for Venture Production, *The Guardian*, 18 March, www.theguardian.com/business/2009/mar/18/centrica-hostile-bid-venture-production (archived at https://perma.cc/8VZH-N8RN)

O'Hara, D (2017) The intrinsic motivation of Richard Ryan and Edward Deci, *American Psychological Association*, 18 December, www.apa.org/members/content/intrinsic-motivation (archived at https://perma.cc/RXB3-H36X)

Tech Monitor (2019) Fiserv snaps up First Data in $22B deal to create fintech powerhouse, 17 January, https://techmonitor.ai/leadership/digital-transformation/fiserv-first-data (archived at https://perma.cc/4PGX-93VH)

United States Securities and Exchange Commission (2006) Sprint Nextel Corporation, www.annualreports.co.uk/HostedData/AnnualReportArchive/s/NYSE_S_2005.pdf (archived at https://perma.cc/Z6PX-CSTT)

Woodsworth, A and Penniman, D (2013) *Mergers and Alliances: The wider view*, Emerald Group Publishing, Bingley

Conclusion: The future of the deal

Why deals will be done, how technology will change them, and who or what will be in the driver's seat

Thank you for sharing our journey so far; we hope it has been an enjoyable and insightful ride. Up to this point, we have looked in detail at each stage of the deal process and how technology is helping dealmakers to address the key challenges that they present. Now, in our concluding chapter, we look to the challenges ahead and examine how deal people and deal technology can work together to find new solutions and better outcomes. We'll also be returning to our central paradox: how technology is reshaping deals and the people who do them, yet at the same time making those dealmakers' human qualities even more critical to deal success.

Let's look first at what will happen to the future volume of deals, given all the changes we've discussed in the book, then we will consider the impact of technologies in each of the deal processes, and then finally examine the crucial role that people will still play.

Why deals will remain vital

The business world has never been short of people willing to predict the future. Cynics may note that many of these prophecies align a little too neatly with particular products and services being sold. For example, few ice cream makers forecast bad weather and not too many car manufacturers announce that we will all be using more public transport in the years ahead.

So, given our authors' 'skin in the game' when it comes to M&A, readers may have some reservations about our first prediction: deals will remain a key and increasingly crucial way for businesses to get ahead and stay ahead in a rapidly changing world. But we believe that our reasons are both sufficiently strong and firmly grounded to stand up to close inspection and withstand any charges of self-interest.

Long-term deal drivers

First, it's worth pointing out that we are talking about fundamental drivers and multi-year trends, not short-term peaks and troughs. While the M&A industry can often seem to be obsessed with measuring deal numbers across short periods, typically quarters and years, then examining what lies behind any movements, the reality is that such analysis, though often engaging and interesting, can be largely meaningless. For example, even without the economic and political shocks caused by the war in Ukraine, simple logic dictated that the dealmaking numbers in 2022 would likely fall from their 2021 highs. The main reason? The 2021 calendar year included a strong element of catch-up as many deals were delayed or halted by the earlier stages of the Covid-19 pandemic. We provided evidence for this in our introductory chapter, with research by BCG (Kengelbach et al, 2020) showing that for deals over $500 million, the typical monthly volume is around 50 deals, but this fell to less than 20 per month at the height of the pandemic. Clearly, almost regardless of other factors, there was then a lot of ground to make up in 2021, boosting deal numbers and hence making it highly likely that 2022, with no catching up to do, would see comparatively lower activity levels.

Yet, most analyses of the year focused on how geopolitical shocks, supply chain pressures and economic uncertainty around everything from inflation to interest rates were behind the fall in deal numbers in 2022. While acknowledging that all those factors are likely to be influential, we believe that it is the underlying drivers that really shape dealmaking across the world, such as the critical need for ongoing strategic change, as just mentioned. And we think that these factors will continue to drive deals and change the types of deals done in the future despite, or even due to, whatever economic and geopolitical shocks lie ahead. Those key drivers include the following:

TECHNOLOGY SEALS DEALS

It will come as no surprise to those who have read this far that we see technology as one of the main drivers for deals in the future (see Chapter 1 for the fullest explanation of how this has evolved so far). The pace of technological change will continue to accelerate, supported by faster computer chips, improved storage, better software and greater interconnectivity. It will remain central to companies across all sectors wanting to maintain their market positions and drive digital and business transformations. Given this centrality, more companies will turn to M&A as a faster track to achieving their strategic objectives, preferring it to other routes such as developing the required skills and technology in-house. Technology-driven deals will take a number of forms, from the standard acquisition of a cutting-edge tech business to partnerships and joint ventures, perhaps on a 'try-before-you-buy' basis in the form of stakes in early-stage projects and companies.

MEETING CUSTOMER NEEDS AND EXPECTATIONS

Delivering to the evolving needs and expectations of customers, brought up on frictionless B2C consumer apps and near-instant fulfilment, will require even the best B2B businesses to acquire greater capabilities, from readymade systems to talented teams. Given the key role of technology in meeting consumer expectations, this will significantly overlap with the previously described driver.

CLIMATE AND ESG CHANGE THE TEMPERATURE FOR DEALS

From acquiring innovators to divesting high-carbon activities, adapting to the climate agenda will continue to drive deals. With the future path of entire technologies, from energy storage solutions to hydrogen power to carbon capture, yet to be fully established, outcomes will vary from exponential growth to rapid obsolescence, but the rewards will help to maintain risk appetite.

But it's important to understand that climate change, as important as it is, will only be one aspect of the ever-broadening ESG agenda, which is increasingly the focus of investors, consumers and governments. This will create multiple – and sometimes competing – drivers to do deals, which we expect to generate a sizeable level of future M&A activity. First, the climate agenda (the E part of ESG) will see companies rationalizing and divesting current assets and acquiring new greener ones. Second, in relation to the S and G parts of ESG, firms will look to improve in areas such as diversity and societal impact and therefore will likely consider purchasing new capabilities and skills, as well as reviewing their governance structure and operating models to ensure that they are measuring, facilitating and, critically, delivering against the required objectives.

BRAINS AND CHAINS: WHY PEOPLE AND SUPPLIERS WILL BE IN DEMAND

The idea that 'our people are our most important asset' is hardly a new one but it is increasingly moving from a slogan to a statement of fact. Many skills, particularly those relating to new and emerging technologies and how they can be applied, are in short supply. With the demand for such skills rising at pace and the pipeline long as well as narrow, buying a 'brain-rich' company is likely to become a key way to acquire talent.

While we tend to think of supply chain pressures in relation to short-term disruption, caused by everything from Covid-19 outbreaks to military conflicts to climate impacts, there are a number of longer-term drivers for dealmaking in this particular area. Scarred by product and staff shortages and delays, companies are seeking to build greater resilience and control by either owning the most crucial elements of their supply chain and/or bringing them closer geographically. So some outsourced activities will be in-sourced through the acquisition of the previously independent supplier. At the same time, companies are concerned about the impact of suppliers on their wider business, from ESG factors to financial and reputational risk, which is another driver of in-sourcing as it allows tighter control over those factors. Finally, disruptive technologies will continue to create major changes to established supply chains (such as, for example, the automotive sector, where everything from electrification to a shortage of semiconductor chips is impacting production), forcing manufacturers to reshape, buy or divest.

DEAL BLOCKERS AND STOPPERS

It's only fair to acknowledge that there are also mitigating factors that could work against the positive drivers just described:

- Antitrust regulatory interference – increased scrutiny of deals on the grounds of competition unfairness and/or national security concerns could significantly hinder deals and impact the M&A process.
- Protectionist policies – fears of rising protectionism across international markets, increasingly driven by cybersecurity and supply chain concerns, could put the brakes on cross-border deals, with the latter being of particular concern to countries that are resource-poor.
- Technology pushback – public, government and workforce concerns over the impacts of new technology on jobs could hinder technology adoption and stop deals.

Interestingly, all these points are connected to what could be described as the apparent retreat or retraction of globalization. This is resulting in commercial pressures, such as the need to reshore supply chains to ensure resilience and just-in-time manufacturing, as well as political imperatives, such as the perceived need by governments to resist overseas bidders for national assets.

The big picture

In order to cope with all the various factors mentioned so far in this chapter, companies must be agile and willing to adapt their strategy, while remaining true to their core values/vision. Deals will be the quickest way to achieve that because they can provide the key capabilities, the people and the access to markets, faster. The other alternatives (like organic growth and joint ventures) will likely be too slow, with 'doing nothing' rightly regarded as being a recipe for ultimate failure. We also believe that the trend described earlier in the book towards roll-up and bolt-on strategies, typically featuring larger companies acquiring smaller add-ons, will continue as established players look to plug gaps and add new capabilities in response to constantly changing markets.

How deals will be done in the future

This is where we explore the growing role of deal technology. Given some of the complexities in this area, let's start with a simple fact and also seek counsel from Ben Harrison, co-founder of deal funding and sourcing platform DealCloud, which was acquired in 2018 by Intapp, a leading global provider of software solutions for professional and financial services firms. Ben has a deep understanding of the current role of technology in M&A, as well as having a front row seat in seeing its future potential (which we will cover later in this chapter).

The simple fact referred to two paragraphs earlier is that, with deals essential to future success, the need to make the process more efficient and effective is likely to intensify. It's clear that technology will therefore have an even greater role to play – the real questions are what that role will be and how it will impact deals and the people who do them. It's also worth noting that dealmakers will be looking for a lot more from technology than efficiencies. For example, as we've discussed in the book, they need the new machine learning and AI capabilities to identify new markets and customer needs. That's because, as buyers step out of their comfort zone and into unfamiliar sectors and geographies to do deals, acquirers will need technology that will also help them to reduce risk and drive better outcomes – from choosing the right target to paying the right price and achieving the desired synergies.

Technology adds pressures too

Looking at it another way, technology is also going to make the pressures on dealmakers a whole lot worse. According to a recent report by Accenture, more than half (52 per cent) of companies doing deals described themselves as primarily acquiring digital companies or assets (perhaps driven to do so by another of the report's findings: 85 per cent of executives said that they were not very confident that their current operating model could meet shifting strategic priorities) (Albert et al, 2021).

But this focus on actively acquiring digital companies brings an additional layer of complexity, because such deals can be more challenging, typically happening faster and requiring different types of closing arrangements and agreements. For example, according to the same Accenture report, software deals close on average a third faster than non-software deals.

So, not only are there more deals ahead, they are going to be more strategically vital, often with more challenging deal processes and integrations – and all will be happening quicker. So, yet again, the only way to square this circle, other than to recruit and rapidly train thousands more dealmakers, will be to use the digital tools and technology that can help existing dealmakers act faster without any loss of trust, relationship and insight.

But before we look at how and where that technology will be applied during the deal process, it's important to understand the particular and sometimes peculiar world of M&A. As Ben Harrison explains, he co-founded DealCloud specifically because, after several years working in M&A as an investment banking analyst and then as a private equity investment professional, he realized that 'the technologies we were using in dealmaking weren't really built for, or fit for, the purpose. It was a square peg in a round hole.' What he means is that the sort of technology he was using had not been built for (let alone by) dealmakers; they were generic tools created for typical commercial organizations. Put simply, they weren't fit for purpose. The fact that, despite these failings, they were still fairly widely used demonstrates how badly they were needed. It also suggests that there is huge potential for uptake, once the right tools are in place.

Deal technology and the human factor

We'll hear more from Ben on the specifics later but it is worth bearing in mind at this stage that applying technology to dealmaking is not likely to have much uptake or impact unless it addresses the very specific needs of the people and processes involved. That's because, as Ben confirms, it's still very much about people and intellectual capital, relationships and trust. Any technology that does not recognize the importance of those factors will, no matter how smart, never really change the future of dealmaking.

One aspect that highlights this point is around the sharing of information and data. Or, to be more precise, the balance between the sharing of information, which is vital to enable the whole deal team to operate efficiently, and the need to respect the proprietary nature of the individual dealmakers' knowledge and relationships built up over years. A 'rainmaker'-type deal professional, who keeps all their information and contacts to themselves, leaving their team and indeed the wider organization in the dark, has clear drawbacks. But equally, hard-won contacts and a bank of insights should be recognized, valued and protected from inappropriate use. As an interesting parallel, one of the major failures of company-wide CRM systems over the years is that senior individuals have not fully participated because they had major concerns that if others in the firm knew more about their contacts then there would be no control over the communication with those contacts.

Good technology will understand and adapt to that particular issue and bad technology will fail to do so. As Ben explains, DealCloud technology has 'solved a lot of those issues so that we have the ability to manage data in a way where you can protect personal relationships and information that is very sensitive and meaningful to people.' We'll return to this subject when we look at the all-important people aspect of future deals later on, but it's important to note that any future deal technology must work with the flow, not against it.

The broad path for deal technology

The rise of technology – particularly data analytics, cybersecurity, machine learning and AI broadly interpreted – has already started to disrupt all parts of the M&A deal process, with global dealmakers adopting new technological tools such as deal automation, natural language processing and big data analytics to select targets and conduct more extensive due diligence. These tools make it possible to analyse vast amounts of structured and unstructured data, as well as speed up M&A processes and better identify hidden risks. Although many advisers have only just started to test these technologies and integrate them into their daily operations, the visible gains will encourage the broader market to place technology at the centre of dealmaking in the coming years. Overall, we can see that the first few stages of the deal process are likely to be more tech-enabled than the latter. This is driven by the fact that the early stages – particularly around testing strategies, identifying targets and conducting due diligence – are typically more data-intensive.

The latter stages of dealmaking become less and less driven by data (and therefore technology), ending with integration, which is perhaps the most human-centric stage of all.

The simple logic behind this is that as a company progresses through the deal stages it becomes more and more about individual relationships. However, there is a significant caveat: throughout our book we have seen how the ability of technology to take on 'human' tasks is seriously underestimated and may therefore, as we will examine, have the most scope for future progress. So it should come as no surprise to the reader that we believe there is still a large role for technology to play in improving the later stages of the dealmaking process.

The future deal process stage by stage

The first two chapters of this book, *Strategy or bust* and *Identify your target*, examined the actual and potential use of technology to test and model strategy, then execute it by identifying potential targets. Here, the ability to sift millions of companies to analyse suitable acquisitions is already highly valuable but is likely to become even more so, particularly as AI is increasingly able to understand the acquirers' individual needs. Technologies like NLP help to access more and richer sources of data to identify those targets and assess their value to the acquirer.

As the need to constantly adapt strategy in response to rapid change across all sectors rises, the pressure to do deals will also rise, increasing the value of deal technology, not only to cope with the number of deals involved, but also to reduce risk. Here deal technology's ability (as discussed in Chapter 1) to balance or even eliminate some of the negative aspects of human behaviours and biases will be crucial. To give just one example, as explored in Chapter 1, gut instinct can undoubtedly be a great thing in the dealmaking environment, but it can, as we showed in that chapter, also lead to unsupported, unchecked and ultra-value destructive decisions.

In addition, as markets and industries cross traditional sector boundaries and fragment, technology is becoming the only way to analyse them effectively. Here, we expect to see the greater adoption of existing technologies, such as those used to map ecosystems as featured in Chapter 2, but with technology's increasing power and capability we see new opportunities to use it to forecast future growth potential.

In Chapter 3, *Winning hearts, minds and money*, we saw how the standardization and digitization of deal information, including common performance metrics, has allowed technology to play a valuable role in widening the market for a seller. Paradoxically, this has actually increased the value add of advisers, who can leverage this information to attract more potential buyers and then manage those buyers to maximize competition and sale price, while also honouring the wishes of the seller in terms of the future direction and integrity of the company. As finance functions evolve, the ability to 'plug into' these sorts of sales 'platforms' will increase, perhaps with the potential to link in with the earlier stages of the deal process, enabling strategists to 'see through' to potential acquisitions and their availability.

Negotiations and pricing (the latter covered in Chapter 4, *Priced to perfection*) are fascinating fields for the application of advanced technologies, which encroach into areas previously identified as largely requiring and benefiting from human attributes. As our interviews on this subject reveal, there is a paradox: in fact, humans are often poor at negotiations. As received wisdom is challenged and huge inroads are made into the development of AI-powered pricing and negotiation tools, this is an area where we believe deal technology adoption can accelerate rapidly.

A closer look at due diligence

As discussed in Chapter 5, *Taking care of business*, due diligence is an area where deal technology first took hold as virtual data rooms replaced the traditional dusty repositories full of paperwork. That made sense because the information within them was data-rich and therefore more easily digitized. It also needed to be shared, but in a highly secure way, which is again easily doable digitally with the right controls in place. But the real driver for digital due diligence was speed, primarily in its ability to handle huge quantities of data, and we've just explained how the need for speed is accelerating. So when you put all those factors together, it seems clear that due diligence is at the top of the list for a technological makeover.

But don't take our word for it. According to a report from Datasite (2020), due diligence is the deal stage that could be most enhanced most by new technologies and digitization. Most practitioners expect technology to enable greater analytical capability and security in the diligence process over the next five years, placing the greatest faith in AI and machine learning technologies to speed it up. Further support comes from a Mergermarket report (Acuris Studios staff and Bite Investments, 2022), which reveals that due diligence scored highest as an area for future investment where digitalization investment is needed and/or would provide the most benefit.

With most of the technology required to digitize and automate further aspects of due diligence already tried and tested, the adoption curve could be a steep one. Adding to lift-off in this area could be the fact that it is perhaps not the most people-friendly area of the deal process. With no disrespect to the many due diligence professionals and the vital importance of their role as part of the M&A process, it's not always considered to be the most exciting area of the deal and many dealmakers would rather spend their time on what they consider to be the more value-additive elements of the deal process.

But, before we get too carried away, it's important to acknowledge that any errors, omissions or issues ignored during the due diligence process can have huge consequences further down the line. That's a responsibility for which a human, not a computer, must still ultimately be held accountable, and indeed will be held responsible by the governmental regulators, should the deal attract their attention.

As we noted in Chapter 6, *Selling the story*, communication is of critical importance from the very start to the very end of any merger, acquisition or corporate restructuring. While communication is a vital tactic and tool during the deal process, at its heart is the underlying factor of reputation, not just of the acquirer but also of those involved with the target company. In terms of its potential for automation, reputation is currently and probably always will be a hard concept to digitalize. However, new technologies will assist with maintaining or even enhancing the standing of anyone or any company engaged in mergers or acquisitions.

Drawing conclusions

We'll leave the final and most human-focused stage of the deal – integration – for our discussion on deal people, but what have we concluded so far? First, that we are still looking at improvements to existing stages rather than fundamental changes to the deal process itself – even though we challenged ourselves at the start of writing this book to test the thesis of whether a sea change will occur in the deal process. And to make sure we weren't biased, we asked this question of each and every one of our expert interviewees, both directly and indirectly. None of our contributors felt that the overall process would change, but they did feel that the stages themselves would.

And even the area most ripe for technology takeover, due diligence, will still need human input and oversight, as we've noted. Don't forget that, as we discussed in Chapter 5, the need to include more and more items in the due diligence process – from regional conflicts and ESG to culture and digital assets – means that just as technology looks able to take care of more of the burden, that burden is getting bigger and bigger.

What we can foresee, however, is the potential of technology not only to speed up individual stages of the deal process, but to connect them better and perhaps, eventually, seamlessly.

With the right information and tools in place, dealmakers could have oversight, even if it's more of a sketch initially, of the whole process. That would enable them to flag up any warning signs early and take the learnings from each stage into the next. This could be the real gamechanger because, currently, there is a tendency to focus on one stage of the deal process at a time, often using separate teams to, for example, source deals, negotiate price, carry out due diligence and manage the post-deal integration process. Missing out on the important connections between, for example, what you pay and how much value you can create post-merger, or measuring integration barriers as part of due diligence, means that a lot more value could be captured.

And a final word on technology

It is always difficult in a book like this to strike the right balance between going into the technical detail and ensuring wider readability. But we particularly liked Ben Harrison's simple but up-close and knowledgeable description of the 'three layers of technology' that the DealCloud platform leverages to support dealmakers, so we are going to share them here. The first is 'the software layer', which he describes as being mainly about user experience, providing simple access to the functions the customer wants. Although we might often think of this as the 'icing on the cake', Ben sees it as a vital cog in the chain and one which requires huge feedback-driven investment to develop it in line with evolving customer expectations and needs.

Next is the 'data layer'. Ben explains that 'everybody wants market data in their system but doesn't want to go searching for it or entering it in a database anymore, so our software model ingests many different third-party market data feeds.' That enables DealCloud, according to Ben, to add value by instantly pulling out data from multiple sources on any company or aspect, such as the key people within it and their broader networks. It's not a huge step from there to apply AI to employee, customer and supplier reactions to previous deals to not only predict the likelihood of post-deal integration success but also to inform how that integration should be designed and managed. Another example would be to use past experience to predict when a company may be likely to come up for sale, based not only on its previous behaviours but also those of other similar businesses, while also incorporating changes in the broader business and competitive environment that may influence the likelihood of a company coming up for sale.

Ben describes the third layer as all about 'integration', by which he means the need to integrate his company's data and tools with those of the customer organization. 'In the customer relationship you must integrate the technology stack so the data flows in the organization and it's not sitting in silence,' he explains. What's fascinating about this explanation is how we authors (and perhaps our readers too) tend naturally to focus on that middle layer of data and analysis, while our expert Ben understands that the actual uptake depends just as much, if not more, on the useability of the software that he provides. He explains this with a comment that we would all do well to remember: 'As humans we love technology, but often hate using business applications that might not be fit for purpose.' In the case of M&A, what he means by this is that the idea of technology doing our 'heavy lifting' is extremely attractive but, unless the user experience is right, no one is going to use it until they absolutely must. This is the perfect sentiment on which to move to our final section of this final chapter, which is about the people aspects of the deal.

Who will do deals in the future?

Given the title of our book it's fitting that, paradoxically, we believe that one of the biggest impacts of technology will be on the role and indeed nature of the people who do deals.

Closing the gap: how the end of information asymmetry is redefining dealmaking

The basis for our thesis is a very simple one: the end of information asymmetry. Deals traditionally took place in a world where few were allowed 'behind the curtain' to meet the key players and access the very time-sensitive and indeed 'secret' files. If that evokes images of Cold War espionage, it's deliberate. This has been a world where only the most confident and best-connected players could operate successfully. Yet even those privileged players would not have access to the whole truth or full facts, so high-stakes bluffing and risk taking were the norm, often based on gut instinct as much as reason. And if that also evokes images of late-night poker games then that is deliberate. As explained in Chapter 5, technology has helped to close that information gap, with profound effects on dealmakers, which we think have not yet fully played through.

The reason for this is that, once the so-called secret information is accessible and shareable, it's less about tight-lipped alpha types staring each other down across the negotiating table but everyone working together to a mutually beneficial outcome. In a nutshell, in a world of shared data, the 'rainmaker' is no longer a 007-like free agent, 'licensed to deal', they are just one part of a wider team. A very important side benefit of this will be the improved diversity of individuals engaged in the deal process, which we will discuss later and which should naturally result in better deal outcomes.

The future of the firm: from rainmaker to robo-adviser?

Let's get a fresh take on this from Ben Harrison at DealCloud, who describes how technology 'captures the information that might have been held by one or two individuals and delivers it back to the organization as an asset on a systematic basis.'

That highlights a potential flaw in the traditional structure of many of the large adviser firms, which theoretically operated as one unit but in reality were dependent on one or more key individuals who brought in big deals without necessarily pooling knowledge and experience. The risk is you're part of a franchise with one brand but you're actually in competition inside your organization. That model clearly had problems even in the days of information asymmetry but at least could then be explained away as a necessary – and in the minds of some, unavoidable – evil. Now it is clearly obsolete. Or is it? After all, the growth of advisory firms remains predicated on hiring and developing people who have or can build strong individual relationships with key people/clients, and we don't expect this to change.

Ben navigates the paradox perfectly: 'Those individuals make a lot of money for their firm but the question is just how much throughput can they do? Can you create efficiencies for those people so they can do work quicker and get better outcomes but still have great client service and institutionalize the firm's knowledge?'

The answer is yes, but only if those individuals accept that the world has moved on and that technology and information are key. 'Harness the key individuals' intellectual capital, then serve it up to all the dealmakers in the organization to help them make better decisions, win more business and drive superior client outcomes,' concludes Ben.

Play nicely: why collaboration is key

So, that shapes our belief that collaboration, both on a human level and in terms of sharing data, will be key to future success. This will enable dealmakers to cope with both the sheer volume of deal work and the need to create better outcomes for buyers and sellers.

We've also seen throughout the book how the silo-ing of the different stages of the deal process leads to unfavourable outcomes. For example, if the people negotiating the price don't communicate with the due diligence team then they may well end up paying too much. And if due diligence isn't conducted with an eye to future integration, then any barriers to integration won't be properly factored into the deal price. This has always been a problem with acquisitions and mergers and is one of the reasons that many deals fail. As Ben explains, 'If you're operating in a silo, you are probably not going to get the best outcome,' adding that 'if you use a broader network and broader information you can drive better outcomes.'

While that may seem like merely an interesting observation about the way deal advisory firms and corporate deal teams are run, its implications, we believe, are far wider. That collaboration not only creates a better chance of working more effectively, pooling resources and joining up the dots to create better deal outcomes (driven by everything from more comprehensive, better-informed target searches to prepared change teams ready to hit the ground on day one, post-merger), it changes the whole culture of dealmaking. We think that one of the best definitions of culture is that 'it's what an organization rewards you for'. So, if dealmakers are rewarded in the future for collaboration not individualism, it by definition changes the culture. Indeed, two of our authors confirm that when they recruited new people into their dealmaking teams post-pandemic, 'the ability to collaborate was a key requisite'.

The future of talent

Talking of recruitment, it's worth noting that we've often talked about the war on talent in terms of a deal driver, but it's also very important to the future of dealmaking itself.

Until recently, investment banks and the big advisory firms have by and large had their pick of those graduating, but there is no room for complacency in this area. Indeed, Ben believes the lack of purpose-built technology represents a potential recruiting threat to the dealmaking profession as younger generations, having grown up with frictionless consumer technology, could be attracted more to working for the big tech companies and put off by M&A firms' heritage of manual process, or, as Ben puts it more colloquially, lumpy 'work stacks', meaning the legacy tools and systems used within the dealmaking/finance industries.

He believes that losing the 'first pick' of talent would be a potentially huge disadvantage because dealmakers need exceptional qualities. 'You must be curious and have a voracious appetite for learning because you often need to gain understanding of a new company or business model with each new mandate,' Ben explains.

We also sense another related threat to the dealmaking establishment. That those tech companies, with the talent at their disposal, could become the dealmakers of the future, leaving the established players behind. If that sounds far-fetched bear in mind that many of the big tech players are already experienced dealmakers with their own venture capital funds and leading-edge tools. Note as well how tech companies have been disintermediating traditional industries such as retail banking, credit card payments and even grocery delivery.

So in summary, dealmaking will still require the best people and must work hard to continue to attract them, but team members will need to be more collaborative and more focused on collective rather than individual targets. Rather than worrying about employees' technology skills, the M&A industry should focus on its own technology systems, because the easier those systems are to use, the more people will want to use them and the more likely they will be to join and build their careers at dealmaking firms.

Driving diversity

That future talent will most certainly be more diverse, as mentioned earlier. Not only because it is right that dealmakers should reflect the society that they operate within but also because, as the sun sets on the days of the stereotypical alpha dealmaker, more diverse thinking is going to be needed and an environment created where it can flourish.

Those previously excluded from the process by unsociable hours and a culture of 'presentee-ism', such as those with caring responsibilities or with particular physical and mental needs, are now able to play a bigger part. With travel to physical meetings all over the world now far less common, virtual working now the norm for many, and greater flexibility over 'office' hours firmly established, the path ahead looks altogether more inclusive.

This may prove to be a virtuous circle, as a more collaborative approach changes culture, which in turn draws in more collaborative and diverse people, who in turn create greater collaboration and diversity.

Summing up

One thing we can say for sure is that although the make-up of the people in the dealmaking industry may be changing, they remain necessary. Or, as our Chapter 5 interviewee, Ashish Agarwal, the former senior vice president, strategy and corporate development at global computer security software company McAfee, neatly puts it: 'I am never ever going to say that we have reached peak technology, but I don't think we will ever replace human interaction. People are investing money in what you will deliver to them, so they will always want to understand your ideas and your thought processes.'

In fact, everyone that we talked to for this book, technologist or otherwise, agrees that doing deals ultimately depends on a combination of human intellectual capital, an ability to build trusted relationships and a willingness to make decisions that, no matter how thorough the preparation, will always be something of a leap of faith.

But none of that means technology will only ever have a minor part to play. It can enable those human elements to be even more effective through enabling a larger number of deals to be done more quickly and providing greater insights that result in better deals that drive superior outcomes.

Protecting us from ourselves: can technology also help us be less human?

Technology can also have a vital role in mitigating our human failings. It's commonly understood that one of the main causes of obesity is that when humans evolved, food was in short supply so our brains were wired to consume as much as possible whenever we could.

Similarly, our hunter-gatherer brains encouraged us to take risks based on limited information, because there was no way to get the full picture in most situations. If we hadn't developed that way, we might never have explored new lands, found new food sources, or encountered new potential partners. Yet, thousands of years later, despite no longer stalking prey for our daily dinner, with transport to take us everywhere and regulations seemingly applied to every aspect of life, we still retain those now generally unhelpful tendencies to eat whenever we can and act on impulse. But technology *is* evolving and, as it does, it will play a growing role in addressing those human failings. For example, technology's ability to process vast seas of data in seconds will help us to continue acting quickly and decisively, but now with greater certainty and definitely more safely.

Much of the traditional culture of dealmaking aligns with one of our innate but irrational beliefs that successful negotiation must always involve a face-off from which only one winner can emerge (despite often claiming that the result was a win-win). With some of the applications of technology discussed in this book, we believe that this concept should be gently retired. To prove this point with just one example, remember that software will help to save billions of dollars left on the table from many deal negotiations (see Chapter 3 for more on this subject).

All together now: how integration is the ultimate prize

The biggest hope and our most optimistic prediction of all is that the power of technology will at last enable the dealmaking profession to overcome the highest hurdle of all: successful integration.

This prediction is built on two foundations. One, that the current form of dealmaking creates a huge 'to do' list that keeps dealmakers so fully occupied that anything not requiring immediate action gets left for later. Or, perhaps more accurately, left until 'too late', because once the deal is done and the integration process begins, there is often great difficulty and cost in making changes, leaving the chance of success slimmer than it should be.

The other foundation to our prediction about integration success is a more cultural one. Historically, it has been the pursuit and capture of the target that has been seen as the heat, heart and 'red meat' of the deal to those that set the tone within the profession. More 'fluffy' areas like measuring the cultural fit of the companies or even inviting the CTOs to assess systems integrations are at worst seen as 'for wimps' and at best as a can to be kicked down the road.

Clearly, this approach is short-sighted, because integration is both the initial driver (after all, why target a company in the first place unless you think it's a good fit?) and the end result, in terms of the valuable synergies that reward you for all the cost and effort of doing the deal.

What's exciting is how deal technology has the potential to clear away all the obstacles to successful integration: by using computing power to reduce that huge 'to do' list, driving the cultural change towards greater collaboration, and creating powerful 'end-to-end' deal platforms that join up the dots across deal stages, making sure that the initial benefits of the deal, first discussed around the boardroom table, are fully realized.

So, that is our final paradox. The most human-centred stage of all, post-deal integration, is the one that can potentially benefit the most from technology. And ultimately that means not only more efficient deals, but ones with better outcomes for all.

KEY POINTS

- Although deal numbers will go up and down according to short-term factors, several key drivers will mean that M&A will long remain the preferred option for companies wishing to adapt to rapidly changing markets.

- The adoption of deal technology will accelerate, particularly in due diligence but it will be evident throughout the deal process, even in those areas considered to be the most people-centric.

- People will remain central to the deal process because of their intellectual capital and ability to build trust/relationships. However, the attributes they require will change as collaboration becomes key and individual 'rainmakers' play less of a central role.

- The end of information asymmetry means that all deal parties will increasingly have access to the same data, supporting greater collaboration, less 'siloed' deal stages and better outcomes.

References

Acuris Studios staff and Bite Investments (2022) The Tech's Factor: The digitalization of private markets in 2022 and beyond, *ION Analytics Community*, 23 May, https://community.ionanalytics.com/the-techs-factor-the-digitalization-of-private-markets-in-2022-and-beyond (archived at https://perma.cc/G4TZ-JK7V)

Albert, G, Chalfant, C, Duarte, G and Ziemann, T (2021) Digitizing M&A: How digital technologies can help reduce risk and create value faster, *Accenture.com*, 2021, www.accenture.com/t20180410t062514z__w__/us-en/_acnmedia/pdf-75/accenture-strategy-sweetening-deal-digitizing-manda-2018-pov.pdf (archived at https://perma.cc/LF2R-EFM3)

Datasite (2020) The New State of M&A: A global perspective, www.datasite.com/us/en/resources/insights/reports/the-new-state-of-m-a----global-report.html (archived at https://perma.cc/FG6V-AHKG)

Kengelbach, J, Keienburg, G, Degen, D, Söllner, T, Kashyrkin, A and Sievers, S (2020) The 2020 M&A report: alternative deals gain traction, *Boston Consulting Group*, 29 September, www.bcg.com/publications/2020/mergers-acquisitions-report-alternative-deals-gain-traction (archived at https://perma.cc/9S9J-C4FV)

INDEX

ABN Amro 33
access and target identification 63–64
accounting fees 95–96
acquisitions
    acquirers and negotiation(s) 67–87
    programmes 47
    see also Mergers and Acquisitions
Acuris (formerly Mergermarket) 85–86, 165
ADIA (PE consortium) 120
Advent 120
adviser(s) 74–76
    platforms 54
affect heuristic 29
Agarwal, Ashish 119
Agility Works 170
Airbnb 94
AirTouch Communications 99
algorithm matching 53
alpha-male stereotypes 86, 102–104
Amply (start-up) 37
analytics/analytical methods
    AI and behavioural analysis 102–103
    big data and due diligence 3–4
    'double materiality' 95
    future of the deal 182–183, 185
    integration 158, 160
    opportunity/strategy 33–34
    predictive 122
    setting out terms 68
    tools for change/future of the deal 170
annual recurring revenues (ARR) 72–73
antitrust regulatory interference 179
Apple 24
aqui-hires 23
art of the deal 101–104
art and dealmaking 89–108
artificial intelligence (AI) 15–16
    art of the deal price 101
    dangerous human(s) 30–31, 32
    and due diligence 122
    due diligence 129
    eliminating bias/target identification 58–59
    emergent tech valuation 105

future of the deal 182–183
genie analogies 12
importance of humans 6
integration 158
intellectual rigour and investment philosophy 62–63
negotiation(s) 81–86
opportunity and strategy 33–34, 35
social data as currency 60
triggering deals 22
valuation and pricing 102–103
asset monitoring 53
assumptions and integration 154–155
AT&T 10–11, 153–154
auctions 76–77, 89, 91
    see also ceiling price
automation 1–3
    due diligence 125
    see also artificial intelligence
automotive industry 22–23, 26–27, 37–39, 94–95, 105, 110
autonomy 169

bad habits and strategy 40
banks 5, 22, 33, 95
Basquiat, Jean-Michel 89, 91
Bass Diffusion models 125–126
Bayes Business School 49, 113, 137, 151
BC Partners 165
BCG (research group) 7–8, 176
behavioural factors, strategy and 27–30
Bell Atlantic (now Verizon) 99, 153–154
belonging 169
benchmarking tools 124
Beyond Meat 49
bias 28–30, 58–59
big data analytics 3–4, 182–183
    see also analytics/analytical methods
'big picture' thinking 179–180
Binstead, Andrew 75–76
Black Swan Data 31, 59–60, 70
Blankfein, Lloyd 22
body language 103–104
bolt-on(s) 47

Brexit 126
British Petroleum (BP) 35–40, 47, 104–106, 162
Browne, John 36
Buffett, Warren 91–92
business to business (B2B)/business to consumer (B2C) 52–53
Byrne, Anthony 170, 171

CAC (cost to acquire a customer) 72–73
Cadbury 109, 111–112
carbon emissions 35–40
Carnegie Mellon University 101
ceiling price 100–104
Centrica 154
Chargemaster 105
chat rooms 141
chief financial officer (CFO) 135
chief technology officers (CTOs) 171
Citi Global Art Market 89
CITY A.M. 79
ClearFactr 22
climate agenda 177–178
climate change *see* carbon emissions
cloud(s) 22
collaboration 190–191
communication and narrative 133–150
    corporate storytelling 134–137
    problem-solving 137–142
        key drivers 138–139
        and people 139–140
        stakeholders 140–141
        technology platforms 141–142
    professionalism 142–147
    role of 138
    standing out 147–149
competence 169
computational power and due diligence 128
computer security software 119–124
    see also McAfee
conclusions, drawing of 186–187
conferencing 10–11, 79–80, 102, 103–104
confirmation bias 29
consumer products sector 23
contractual difficulties 103
corporate storytelling, rise and fall of 134–137
cost to acquire a customer (CAC) 72–73
costs 72–73, 95–96
    see also pricing
Covid-19 *see* pandemic
CPP Investments (PE consortium) 120
CREATE Fertility 77–80

Crosspoint Capital 120
crucible of change 8–9
CTOs *see* chief technology officers
culture, integration 169
customer needs and expectations 177
customer relationship management (CRM) platforms 70–71, 113, 163, 182
cybersecurity 22, 179, 182–183

data
    big data analytics 3–4, 182–183
    as currency 59–60
    and due diligence 3–4, 109–132
    see also analytics/analytical methods
Datasite 119
Davison, Paul 60–64
deal blockers and stoppers 179
deal costs 72–73, 95–96
deal cycle
    and due diligence 114–115
    integration 151–174
deal drivers
    ESG 49–50
    future of talent 191
    integration 162
    long-term 176–180
deal technology *see* technology
DealCloud 75
debt 95–96
Deci, Edward 169
decision-making and bias 28–30
dialling in synergies 99
Diffbot 129
digital transformation/value 163–164
diversity 86, 192
"double materiality" 95
due diligence 109–132
    big data analytics 3–4
    disruption and age of 112–113
    failure 110–111
    future of the deal 185–186
    'hard/soft factors' 117, 118–119
    need for speed 113–114
    and technology 114–117
        role of 119–124
    virtual coal face 124–129

earnings before interest, taxes, depreciation and amortization (EBITDA) 85–86, 93, 97, 113
earnings before interest and taxes/sales (EBIT/sales) 85–86
earn-outs (integration) 156–157, 159

Eastman Kodak 26–27
ecosystem(s) 47–48
electric vehicles (EV) 26–27, 37, 38–39,
    94–95, 105
empowering of human input 55–56
enterprise resource planning (ERP)
    systems 157, 163, 164
environmental, social and governance (ESG)
    ratings 49, 95, 97–98, 119,
    126–127, 177–178
EQT (global investment organization) 54
European Union, Brexit 126
EY Diligence Edge (benchmarking tool) 124

Facebook 5, 94, 101
'fast fashion' firms 118–119
female CEOs 85–86
Fintech companies 160
First Data 160
Fiserv, Inc 160
forbes.com 58–59, 114
fragmentation of the marketplace 50–51
FTSE 100 insurers 136–137
future of the deal 175–196
    stage by stage 183–188

Geis, George 114
gender 85–86, 102–104
Gender Diversity and Dealmaking 2022
    85–86
General Motors 94–95
GIC (PE consortium) 120
global pandemic *see* pandemic
Goldman Sachs 5, 22
Gove, Michael 126
'greenwashing' 49–50
gut feeling 26–27, 29, 31, 184, 189
    emergent tech valuation 105–106
    human advantage over machines 84
    pandemic 8
    and strategy 21–43

'happy ever after' 17, 80, 134, 135,
    138, 139
'hard factors', due diligence 117, 118–119
Headland 142–147
Hecker, Jean Xavier 95
Heritage, Ross 165–168, 171–172
heuristics 29
Hollywood narratives 135, 136, 141–142
Holt, Carrie Anne 165–168, 171–172
hubris hypothesis 30
human connection

due diligence 121
    integration 160–164
human factor
    advantage over machines 84
    future of the deal 182–183
human instinct
    and strategy 21–43
    see also gut feeling
human judgement and due
    diligence 109–132
human resources (HR)
    bad habits, strategy and 40
    integration 156, 171
hybrid approaches/negotiation(s) 84–85

identifying targets *see* target identification
IFS (software company) 75–76
illusion of control 29
importance of humans 6–7
in vitro fertilisation (IVF) 77–80
INEOS 39
inferred behaviours 127
information asymmetry 189
information availability bias 29
information gap and due diligence 119
information and target identification 63–64
initial public offerings (IPOs) 3, 94, 120
innovation, theory to practice and target
    identification 56–59
insight 144
instinct
    and strategy 21–43
    see also gut feeling
insurers 136–137
integration 151–174
    barriers to 155–160
        bringing down of 158
        earn-outs/TSAs 156–157
        role of technology of 158–159
    complications 152–153
    human touch 160–164
        deal drivers 162
        digital transformation 164
        digital value 163–164
        evolution 162–163
        people's eye view 168–170
    technologists 170–172
    testing of 164–168
    unclear route towards 153
    winners and losers 153–155
        assumptions 154–155
intellectual rigour and investment
    philosophy 62–63

interest payments on debt 95–96
'internet of concepts' 129
investment banking fees 95–96
investment philosophy 62–63
'invisible hand of the market' (Smith) 28
ION Group 165
IPOs (initial public offerings) 3, 94, 120
IQ for Sales (Zoom) 103–104
IVF *see* in vitro fertilisation
IVIRMA Global 77–80

JPMorgan 95

key performance indicators (KPIs) 72–74, 85–86
Kim, J Daniel 139–140
King, Julie 59
King, Steve 31, 59–60, 70
Kraft 109, 111–112

Lane4 Management Group 118, 168
Lawson, Rob 47, 104–106
Lawson, Robert 35–40
legal fees 95–96
Legh, Lucy 142–147
lifetime value (LTV) 72–73
LinkedIn 133–134
lockdowns *see* pandemic
long-term deal drivers 176–180
'look them in the eye' hurdle 116
Looney, Bernard 36
Lotus 1-2-3 33–34
Love Island 67

McAfee 16–17, 119–124
machine learning (ML)
    dangerous human(s) 30–31
    future of the deal 182–183
    genie analogies 12
    pricing 97–98
    technology platforms 54
male CEOs 85–86
Malthouse, Stephen 142–147
material-living 95
Mergermarket (now Acuris) 85–86, 165
Mergers and Acquisitions (M&A)
    bias 28–30
    cash costs 95–96
    communication and narrative 142–147
    difference in deals 2–3
    due diligence 109, 118–119
        deal technology 129
        need for speed 113
        regulation and 111–112

future of the deal 175–196
pressure to do deals 4–5
pricing 90, 94
    future of 104–106
    vagaries of valuation 92
strategy 21
    in action 35–40
    behavioural factors 27–30
    dangerous human(s) 31–32
    and dealmaking 25
    and opportunity 34
target identification
    ESG as deal drivers 49–50
    innovation, theory to practice 56
    multidimensionality of targets 47
technology-driven valuation
    disparities 94
see also negotiation(s)
Microsoft 133–134
    Teams conferencing 10–11, 79–80, 102
ML *see* machine learning
Moneyball (Lewis) 6
Moorhouse, Adrian 17, 118, 168, 169, 170
multidimensionality/target identification 47
multi-model platforms 53
Musk, Elon 26–27, 114, 148–149

Nadella, Satya 133–134
Nargund, Geeta 77–80
narrative, communication and 133–150
natural language generation (NLG) 101
natural language processing (NLP) 3–4, 54, 60, 97–98, 101
need for speed 5–6, 113–114
negotiation(s) 67–87
    adviser roles 74–76
    auctions 76–77
    hybrid 84–85
    key drivers 68–69
    the machine/AI 81–86
    personal business/reproductive health 77–80
    role of 80–81
    setting out terms 68
    standardization 70–74
    and technology 70
    see also Mergers and Acquisitions
net retention rate(s) (NRR) 72–73
Nextel 153–154
NGOs *see* non-governmental organizations
nightmare honeymoons 17
non-governmental organizations (NGOs) 36
non-text sources and due diligence 129

online data as currency 59–60
online message boards 141
opportunity, strategy and 33–35
optimism 29
Orange 118, 168–169
overconfidence/excessive optimism 29

Pactum 81–86
pandemic 1, 7–9
  due diligence 116, 121
  personal business/reproductive health 78
  remote working 39–40
PE *see* private equity
people and supply 178–179
people's eye view, integration 168–170
PepsiCo 49
Permira (PE consortium) 120
personal approaches 78–79
  see also human connection; human factor
pharmaceuticals 22
platforms
  communication and narrative 141–142
  CRM 70–71, 113, 163, 182
  social media 5, 94, 101, 114, 144–146, 148–149
  see also technology
podcasts 129
post-truth world and due diligence 127–128
PR firms and messaging (public relations) 137, 139, 140–141, 144
predictive analytics 122
pressure to do deals 4–6
pricing 89–108
  art of the deal 101–104
  deal costs 95–96
  future 104–106
  gap between value and 91–92
  powered by technology 96–101
  vagaries of valuation 92–95
private equity (PE) and firms 49–50, 54, 57, 120, 142–143
protectionist policies 179
Prudential (FTSE 100 insurer) 136–137

Qui, Tony 56–59, 122–124, 125, 130

radio broadcasts 129
rainmaking 189–190
Rand, Martin 81–86, 105–106
reality shows 67
referenda 126
regulation, due diligence 111–112
remote working 39–40

reproductive health 77–80
reputation 143
research and development (R&D) 135
return on equity (ROE) 85–86
risk
  due diligence 123
  see also bias; due diligence
robo-advisers 189–190
robots *see* artificial intelligence; automation
robust client retention 72–73
Rolls-Royce 110
roll-ups 47
Royal Bank of Scotland (RBS) 33
'Rule of 40' metrics 72–73
Ryan, Richard 169

S&P 500 97–98
Salt, Chris 142
SAP technology 170
scalability metrics 72–73
science of dealmaking 89–108
sealing the deal/technology 177
Self-Determination and Intrinsic Motivation in Human Behavior (O'Hara) 169
seller(s) and negotiation(s) 67–87
setting out terms in negotiation(s) 68
share price performance 85–86
Smith, Adam 28
sniff test(s) 9
social data as currency 59–60
social media platforms 5, 94, 101, 114, 144–146, 148–149
'soft factors', due diligence 117, 118–119
SoftBank Vision Fund 15, 60–64
software-as-a-service (SaaS) 72–73
sophistication and due diligence 128
soundtracks 129
Special Purpose Acquisition Companies (SPACs) 3
Sprint 153–154
SS&C Intralinks 11–12, 85–86, 113
stakeholders
  communication and narrative 140–141, 143, 145
  due diligence 118–119
  personal approaches 78–79
standardization and negotiation 70–74
Star Trek 35, 152
StartX (venture capital fund) 129
stated behaviours 127
stereotypes 86, 102–104
Storonsky, Nik 58–59
Strategic rationale (wind power initiative) 37

strategy 21–43
    in action 35–40
        bad habits 40
        deals on deals 36–38
        new technologies and skills 38–39
        over time 35–36
        remote working 39–40
    behavioural factors 27–30
    dangerous human(s) 30–32
    and dealmaking relationships 23–25
    and integration 167–168
    and opportunity 33–35
    paradox 25–27
    triggering deals 22–23
    see also pricing
success see negotiation(s)
supply and demand 178–179
Symphony Technology Group 120
synergies
    dialling in 99
    due diligence 116–117

T Mobile 168–169
Takeover Code 111–112, 145
talent, future of 191–192
Tao Leadership 170
target identification 45–65
    fund leader(s) and vision 60–64
    and innovation 56–59
        bias and AI 58–59
        growing role of technology 56–57
        preemptively identifying
            targets 57–58
    multidimensionality 46–47
    new dimensions in dealmaking 47–48
    optimal technological
        environments 48–51
    power to the people 64
    social data as currency 59–60
    technology platforms and people 52–56
Teams conferencing (Microsoft) 10–11,
        79–80, 102
technologists, integration 170–172
technology
    alternative energy 35–40
    communication and narrative 139–140
        challenges 144–145
        extending of reach 143–144
        insight 144
        platforms driving change 141–142
        standing out 147–149
    dangerous human(s) 30–32
    and due diligence 114–117
        added due diligence 125–126

barriers to adoption 123
data room(s) 119–120
deal technology 129
evolving role of 128–129
human connection 121
information gap 119
key applications 122
optimising models 123–124
potential of 122–123
role of 119–124
virtual deal revolution(s) 120–121
future of the deal 175–196
    final word 187–188
    human factor 182–183
    pressures 180–181
    pushback 179
    sealing the deal 177
genie analogies 10–13
integration 165–166
    barriers 158–159
    culture 169
    human touch 160–164
    successful example 160
in negotiations 70
    SaaS 72–73
powering pricing 96–101
pricing
    emergent tech valuation 105–106
    to model outcomes 103
    versus testosterone 102–104
remote working 39–40
rise of 11–12
setting strategies 30–32
target identification 45–65
    fund leader(s) and vision 60–64
    and human interaction 62
    and innovation 56–59
    optimal environment 48–51
    people and platforms 52–56
to the rescue 9–13
    platforms, people and
        technology 52–56
triggering deals 22–23
valuation disparities 94
valuation and pricing 102–104
telecoms 10–11, 99, 118, 153–154, 168–169
Tesla 26–27, 94–95
    see also Musk
Thiam, Tidjane 136–137
T-Mobile 118
tools for change, integration 170
tools for contractual difficulties 103
Transition Services Agreements (TSAs) 34,
        156–157, 159, 170–171

trust and reputation 143
TSA *see* Transition Services Agreements
TV reality shows 67
Twitter 114, 144, 148–149

Uber 60–61
uncertainty and ceiling price 100–101
United Kingdom
    Brexit 126
    deal technology and due diligence 129
    Takeover Code 111–112, 145

value/valuation
    digital value/integration 163–164
    future of valuation 95
    methods, valuation 93
    in negotiations 72–73
    and price 91–92
    and technology 102–104
    technology-driven disparities 94
    vagaries of 92–95
vendor due diligence 115
venture capital (VC) 52–53, 58–59, 129

Venture Productions 154
Verizon (formerly Bell Atlantic) 99, 153–154
video conferencing 10–13, 143–144
video soundtracks 129
virtual deal revolution(s) and due diligence 120–121
VitalFields 81
vitalness of deals 175–176
    due diligence 109–132
Vodafone 99
Volkswagen 110

WhatsApp 94
Why Deals Fail & How to Rescue Them (Driessen, Faelten & Moeller) 13
wind farm market 37

Xerox 26–27

Yusaka, Maezawa 90

Zoom conferencing 10–11, 79–80, 102, 103–104